Black's

Rhyming and Spelling Dictionary

Contents

★ Using a rhyming dictionary 4

★ Writing poetry 6

a words ending in a sounds 8

-a to -aced	8-9
-ack to -act	10-11
-ad to -age	12-13
-ale to -air	14-15
-airy to -am	16-17
-ame to -and	18-19
-ane to -ape	20-21
-arch to -asp	22-23
-ass to -ate	24-25
-ator to -ay	26-27
-aze	28

e words ending in e sounds 29

-e	29
-eaf to -ear	30-31
-east to -eck	32-33
-ecks to -edge	34-35
-eece to -een	36-37
-eep to -elp	38-39
-elt to -ent	40-41
-ept to -est	42-43
-et to -eve	44

i words ending in i sounds 45

-i 45
-ib to -iddle 46-47
-ide to -iff 48-49
-ift to -ike 50-51
-ild to -im 52-53
-ime to -ine 54-55
-ing to -ire 56-57
-is to -it 58-59
-itch to -iver 60

o words ending in o sounds 61

-o 61
-oad to -obble 62-63
-obe to -oint 64-65
-oise to -olt 66-67
-ome to -ong 68-69
-oo 70-71
-ood to -oon 72-73
-oop to -ope 74-75
-ore to -ores 76-77
-ork to -ort 78-79
-ose to -ouch 80-81
-oud to -ow 82-83
-ower to -ows 84-85
-oy 86

u words ending in u sounds 87

-ub to -uck 87
-uckle to -ug 88-89
-ul to -ump 90-91
-un to -up 92-93
-ur to -urse 94-95
-urt to -ut 96-97
-ute to -uzzle 98

★ Index 99

Using a rhyming dictionary

Rhymes are everywhere – in greetings cards, in playground games, chanted at football matches, in pop songs... and in many poems.

This rhyming dictionary makes it easier to write a rhyme. It can trigger all sorts of unusual rhyming words. Who would have thought of a chimpanzee smelling a sweet pea? Or of trying to hypnotize in pigsties!

Try flicking through the book for ideas for funny jingles and nonsense rhymes. It will also help you if you are stuck for a rhyme in a serious poem.

Rhyming and spelling

When words rhyme they share the same sound at the end, for example, fig and big. Not all words that rhyme share the same spelling patterns.

In this book you will find rhyming words which are spelled in different ways, although the end part sounds the same. For instance, there are nine different ways to spell the rhyming sound at the end of the word igloo: grew, ewe, two, shoe, you, through, flu, blue.

Poets look at words carefully and use rhymes to create images and make us laugh. As they build up a bank of words which rhyme, they come to know the various possibilities when spelling words. If you keep dipping into this book to create rhymes, it will help your spelling as well.

So what are you waiting for?
Open up this rhyming store.

Who's that on your mobile phone –
a fishbone or an ice cream cone?
Invent yourself a vagabond
and madly wave a magic wand.
Catch yourself a carnivore
dressed up in a pinafore!

Then post your rhyme to a friend –
rhyming words are cool to send...

How to find rhyming words

Use the page headings

★ This dictionary arranges words alphabetically according to their end vowel sounds: a, e, i, o or u.

★ To find words that end with a particular sound, first find the vowel sound (a, e, i, o or u) in the coloured strip at the top of the page, then look for the sound ending, e.g. –ay.

Use the index

★ The index lists words in alphabetical order. To find rhymes for a particular word, first look up that word in the index.

★ If you look up a word such as play, you will find it with a vowel sound after it and a page number: play / –ay 27.

★ On page 27 (see below) is a list of rhyming words with –ay sounds. The list starts with the shortest words and ends with the longest. You can use any of these words to rhyme with play.

★ Other sounds which rhyme with play, but which are spelled differently, are also listed, for example, neigh, prey and ballet.

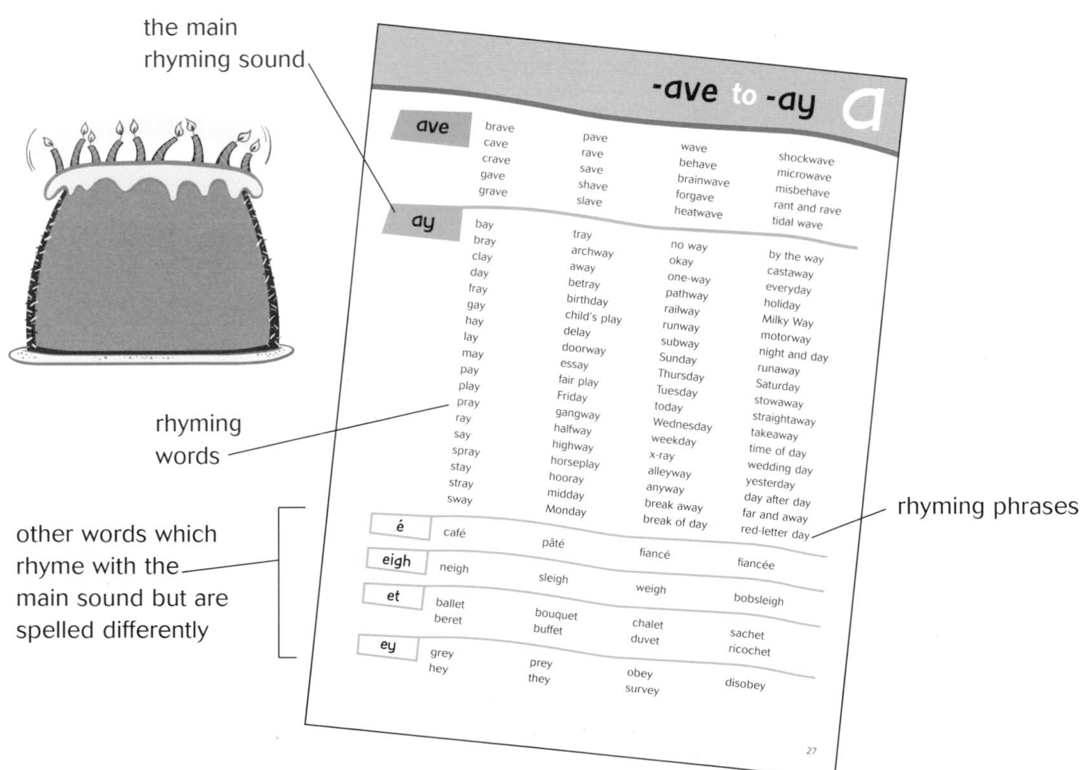

-ave to -ay a

ave
brave, cave, crave, gave, grave, pave, rave, save, shave, slave, wave, behave, brainwave, forgave, heatwave, shockwave, microwave, misbehave, rant and rave, tidal wave

ay
bay, bray, clay, day, fray, gay, hay, lay, may, pay, play, pray, ray, say, spray, stay, stray, sway, tray, archway, away, betray, birthday, child's play, delay, doorway, essay, fair play, Friday, gangway, halfway, highway, horseplay, hooray, midday, Monday, no way, okay, one-way, pathway, railway, runway, subway, Sunday, Thursday, Tuesday, today, Wednesday, weekday, x-ray, alleyway, anyway, break away, break of day, by the way, castaway, everyday, holiday, Milky Way, motorway, night and day, runaway, Saturday, stowaway, straightaway, takeaway, time of day, wedding day, yesterday, day after day, far and away, red-letter day

é
café, pâté, fiancé, fiancée

eigh
neigh, sleigh, weigh, bobsleigh

et
ballet, beret, bouquet, buffet, chalet, duvet, sachet, ricochet

ey
grey, hey, prey, they, obey, survey, disobey

27

Writing poetry

How to create sounds

Many poems use **full rhymes**. These are words which have exactly the same end sound, e.g. smack and black. Some words nearly rhyme and these are called **near rhymes** or **half rhymes**, e.g. slip and sleep. Some words look as if they will rhyme, but actually do not. These are called **eye rhymes**, e.g. cough and through.

In most poems, the rhymes come at the *end* of the line:

Humpty Dumpty sat on a wall.
Humpty Dumpty had a great fall.

Some poems use **internal** rhymes. These come in the *middle* of lines:

The sun spills sunlight,
fills corners with honey...

Rhymes help to bind a poem together and make sentences memorable. You can also use **alliteration** so that words start with the same sound:

The sun spills sunlight...

Using words which sound like their meaning can make a poem really effective. This is called **onomatopoeia**:

The snake hissed.

How to create pictures

You can build pictures in your reader's mind in different ways. Try using **similes** to say that one thing is like another:

The moon was like a smiling face.

Some similes use the word as:

She was quick as an eel.

Metaphors say that one thing is another:

The candyfloss clouds drifted.
(See the poem on page 50.)

Personification brings objects alive:

The trees waved their branches in the wind.

Make words work

When you write poems, choose powerful words. Read this sentence:

The cat went along the wall.

It would be more effective if it used powerful and precise language:

The Siamese limped along the red brick wall.

Try different types of poetry

In this dictionary you will find different types of poetry to inspire you. Have a go at writing your own poems based on the types below.

Haiku *(see pages 33, 45)*
These short poems come from Japan. They are usually three lines long and have a pattern of 5/7/5 syllables. You can also use your own syllable pattern.

Cinquain *(see pages 19, 59)*
These are like haiku. They have five lines and use a pattern of 2/4/6/8/2 syllables. You can also invent your own syllable pattern.

Limericks *(see page 68)*
These are often funny and usually have three long lines and two short ones. The rhyming pattern is aa/bb/a.

Riddles *(see page 28)*
These are fun to write. Try to give clues without giving the subject away.

Acrostics *(see page 91)*
These poems spell out a word in letters hidden somewhere within the lines. You read acrostics downwards.

Calligrams *(see pages 54-55)*
These are written so that the shape of the words reflect the meaning. On page 54 the letters of the words 'rolling pin' form the shape of a rolling pin.

Rhyming couplets *(see page 71)*
These are two lines which rhyme. You can invent other rhyming patterns, as in the poem on page 83, which uses the pattern aa/bb/a.

Word plays *(see pages 41, 93)*
Some poems play with words by taking them literally.

Rhyming games

Pass the rhyme

This is a quick game you can play anywhere. The first player says a word and the next has to say a rhyming word. The rhyming sound is passed on until no-one can think of another rhyming word.

Place names

This is a good game for journeys. Try finding rhymes for place names, or people's names, for example:

I felt loud
in Stroud,
picked my teeth
in Moncrieff...

Copycat

Think of a well-known nursery rhyme or song and copy it, changing some of the words. Look at the alternative version of Humpty Dumpty on page 14.

a -a to -able

a

baa
ha
ma
pa
aha
gaga
grandma
grandpa
ha ha
hoo-ha
hoopla
mama
papa
chihuahua
Panama
tra-la-la

ar

bar
car
far
jar
scar
spar
star
tar
tsar
afar
ajar
all-star
bazaar
crossbar
crowbar
guitar
radar
sitar
so far
towbar
cable car
caviar
handlebar
jaguar
movie star
near and far
superstar
TV star

are

are

ab

blab
cab
crab
dab
drab
fab
flab
grab
jab
lab
nab
scab
slab
stab
kebab
minicab

abble

babble
dabble
gabble
scrabble

abby

crabby
flabby
shabby
tabby

able

able
cable
fable
sable
stable
table
times table
timetable
turntable
unable
unstable
willing and able

abel

label

Carla the baby-faced chihuahua chased Abby the dirty-faced tabby ...

ace

ace, brace, face, grace, lace, pace, place, race, space, trace

airspace, birthplace, deface, disgrace, embrace, fireplace, horse race, lose face, misplace, replace

retrace, sack race, shoelace, snail's pace, unlace, workspace, baby face, commonplace, double-space, face to face

hiding place, human race, in your face, outer space, out of place, pride of place, relay race, saving grace, blue in the face, obstacle race

ase

base, case, chase

bookcase, nutcase, staircase

suitcase, database, just in case

pillowcase, wild goose chase

aced

braced, faced, graced, laced, paced, placed, raced

spaced, traced, barefaced, defaced, disgraced, displaced, embraced

fast-paced, misplaced, outpaced, red-faced, replaced, retraced, shamefaced

straitlaced, two-faced, unlaced, angel-faced, baby-faced, dirty-faced, interlaced

aist

waist

aste

haste, paste

taste, waste

bad taste, good taste

toothpaste, cut and paste

a -ack to -ackle

ack

back, black, crack, hack, jack, knack, lack, pack, quack, rack, sack, shack, slack, smack, snack, stack, thwack, track, whack, attack, backpack, backtrack, bareback, drawback, flapjack, flashback, haystack, hijack, horseback, humpback, hunchback, icepack, laid back, outback, racetrack, ransack, rucksack, setback, sidetrack, soundtrack, switchback, tailback, unpack, wisecrack, answer back, back to back, heart attack, jumping jack, lumberjack, paperback, piggyback, single track, stickleback, Union Jack, clackity-clack, pat on the back

ac

mac, sac, tarmac, bric-a-brac, cul-de-sac, maniac, zodiac, insomniac

ak

yak, kayak, anorak, yakkity-yak

aque

plaque

ackle

cackle, crackle, shackle, tackle, ramshackle

ackal

jackal

Rain smacks
attacks
ramshackle
back streets.
Lightning crackles,
cracks
the glistening back
of the tarmac
night.

acks

cracks
jacks
lacks
packs
quacks
racks
sacks
shacks
smacks
snacks
stacks
thwacks
tracks
whacks
attacks
backpacks
backtracks
flapjacks
haystacks
hijacks
ransacks
rucksacks
setbacks
sidetracks
soundtracks
switchbacks
unpacks
railway tracks

aks

yaks
kayaks
anoraks

ax

fax
lax
max
sax
tax
wax
beeswax
climax
earwax
relax
thorax
candle wax
income tax
to the max

axe

axe
pickaxe
poleaxe
battle-axe

act

act
fact
pact
tact
abstract
attract
compact
contract
distract
exact
extract
impact
react
subtract
artefact
overact
riot act
matter of fact
overreact
put on an act

acked

backed
blacked
cracked
hacked
lacked
packed
quacked
sacked
slacked
smacked
snacked
stacked
thwacked
tracked
whacked
attacked
backpacked
backtracked
hijacked
humpbacked
hunchbacked
jam-packed
ransacked
sidetracked
unpacked
vacuum-packed

a -ad to -ade

ad

bad
clad
dad
fad
glad
had
lad
mad
pad
sad
granddad
kneepad
launch pad
nomad
not bad
Sinbad
too bad
ironclad
mum and dad
not all bad
shoulder pad
Trinidad
stark raving mad

add

add

ade

blade
fade
glade
grade
jade
made
shade
spade
trade
wade
arcade
decade
evade
grenade
handmade
homemade
invade
lampshade
parade
persuade
sunshade
unmade
barricade
cavalcade
centigrade
escapade
fire brigade
lemonade
marmalade
orangeade
ready-made
shoulder blade

aid

braid
laid
maid
paid
raid
staid
afraid
bridesmaid
first aid
mermaid
repaid
unpaid
well-paid
hearing aid
overpaid
underpaid

ayed

brayed
frayed
played
prayed
sprayed
stayed
strayed
swayed
arrayed
betrayed
decayed
delayed
displayed
portrayed
replayed
x-rayed

ede

suede

eighed

neighed
sleighed
weighed
outweighed

eyed

obeyed
preyed
surveyed
disobeyed

aft

craft
daft
graft
raft
shaft
aircraft
crankshaft
life raft
spacecraft
witchcraft
fore and aft
hovercraft

aughed

laughed

aught

draught

ag

bag
brag
crag
drag
flag
gag
hag
lag
nag
rag
sag
snag
stag
swag
tag
wag
air bag
beanbag
chinwag
handbag
jet lag
name tag
postbag
price tag
punchbag
ratbag
sandbag
teabag
windbag
zigzag
doggy bag
hoist the flag
pack your bag
saddlebag
scallywag
sleeping bag

age

age
cage
page
rage
stage
wage
backstage
birdcage
Bronze Age
enrage
front page
Ice Age
offstage
old age
outrage
rampage
rib cage
space age
Stone Age
teenage
upstage
web page
Iron Age
under age

Love poem

I'll be your –
handmade hearing aid,
homemade sunshade,
underpaid barricade.

a -ale

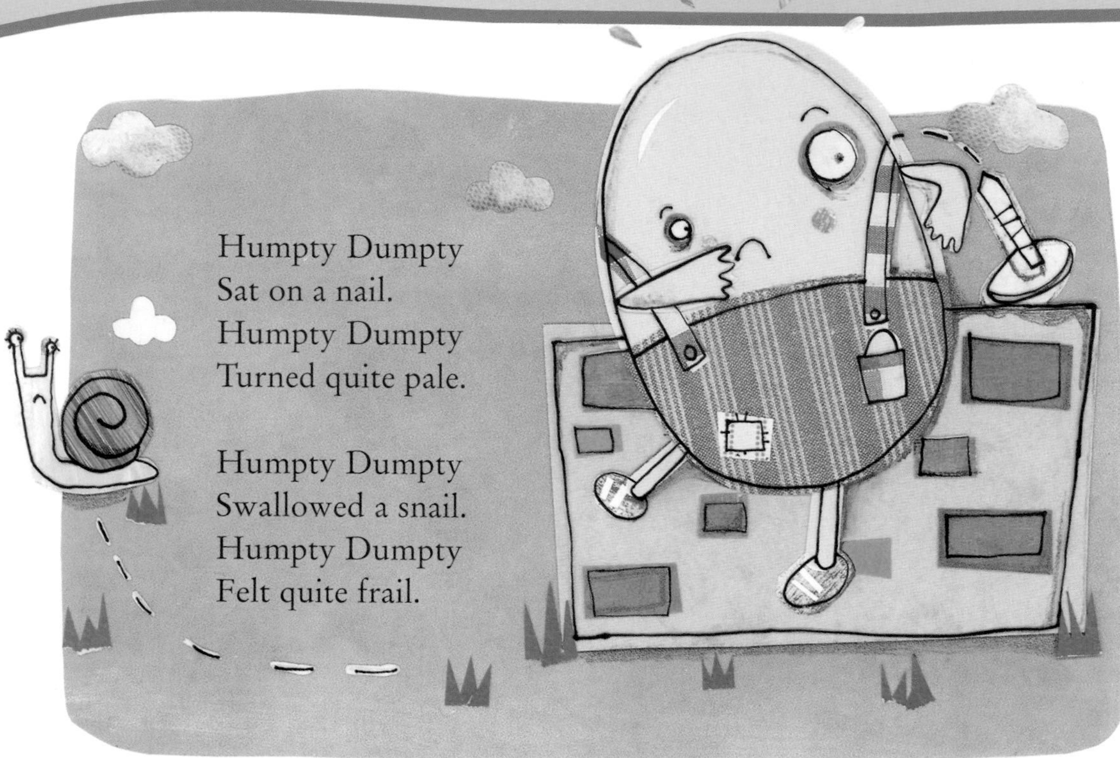

Humpty Dumpty
Sat on a nail.
Humpty Dumpty
Turned quite pale.

Humpty Dumpty
Swallowed a snail.
Humpty Dumpty
Felt quite frail.

ale

ale	sale	female	fairytale
bale	scale	for sale	garage sale
dale	stale	impale	ginger ale
gale	tale	inhale	killer whale
male	whale	telltale	nightingale
pale	exhale	car boot sale	old wives' tale

ail

ail	pail	airmail	toenail
bail	quail	blackmail	fingernail
fail	rail	chainmail	Holy Grail
frail	sail	detail	monorail
hail	snail	e-mail	nature trail
jail	tail	fan mail	ponytail
mail	trail	pigtail	tooth and nail
nail	wail	thumbnail	without fail

air

air	pair	funfair	unfair
chair	stair	highchair	wheelchair
fair	armchair	mid-air	off the air
flair	au pair	pushchair	on the air
hair	despair	repair	rocking chair
lair	éclair	thin air	walk on air

aire

billionaire	millionaire	solitaire

are

bare	hare	square	fanfare
blare	mare	stare	hardware
care	rare	aware	nightmare
dare	scare	beware	prepare
fare	share	bus fare	set square
flare	snare	compare	software
glare	spare	declare	threadbare

ear

bear	tear	nightwear	polar bear
pear	wear	sportswear	teddy bear
swear	footwear	grizzly bear	underwear

eir

heir	their

ere

there	nowhere	anywhere	then and there
where	somewhere	everywhere	neither here nor there
elsewhere	so there!	here and there	

Complete the rhyme

As I was going up the stairs
I met a man with seven bears
Each ..... had six .....
Each ..... had five .....

a -airy to -ake

airy

airy
dairy
fairy
hairy
tooth fairy
airy-fairy
sugar plum fairy

airie

prairie

ary

scary
vary
wary
canary
contrary
unwary

ake

bake
brake
cake
drake
fake
flake
lake
make
quake
rake
sake
shake
snake
stake
take
wake
awake
cheesecake
earthquake
fishcake
fruitcake
grass snake
handbrake
handshake
keepsake
milkshake
mistake
namesake
oatcake
pancake
snowflake
teacake
birthday cake
Christmas cake
double take
give and take
overtake
pat-a-cake
piece of cake
rattlesnake
undertake
wide-awake
for goodness sake

ache

ache
backache
earache
headache
heartache
toothache
bellyache
stomach ache

aque

opaque

eak

break
steak
beefsteak
daybreak
firebreak
heartbreak
jailbreak
outbreak
rumpsteak
tea break
windbreak
make or break
take a break
coffee break
give me a break

all

all, ball, call, fall, hall, pall, small, squall, stall, tall, wall, baseball, birdcall, bookstall, downfall, eyeball, fireball, football, freefall, meatball, netball, nightfall, oddball, phone call, pinball, pitfall, play ball, rainfall, recall, snowball, snowfall, town hall, windfall, all in all, basketball, cannonball, crystal ball, free-for-all, know-it-all, off-the-wall, on the ball, overall, shopping mall, up the wall, volleyball, wall-to-wall, waterfall, fly on the wall

aul

haul, maul, caterwaul, overhaul

awl

bawl, brawl, crawl, drawl, scrawl, shawl, sprawl, trawl

alley

alley, galley, valley, blind alley

ally

pally, rally, tally, dilly-dally

am

am, clam, cram, dam, gram, ham, jam, pram, ram, scam, scram, sham, slam, swam, tram, wham, yam, exam, program, wigwam, anagram, diagram, hologram, in a jam, kilogram, milligram, traffic jam, battering ram

amb

lamb, door jamb

a -ame to -an

ame

blame
came
fame
flame
frame
game
lame
name
same
shame
tame
ball game
became
door frame
nickname
surname
claim to fame
crying shame
overcame
window frame

aim

aim
claim
maim
acclaim
exclaim
proclaim
reclaim
take aim

amp

camp
champ
clamp
cramp
damp
lamp
ramp
scamp
stamp
tramp
foglamp
postage stamp

amper

camper
damper
hamper
pamper
scamper
tamper
picnic hamper

an

ban
bran
can
clan
fan
flan
gran
man
nan
pan
plan
ran
scan
span
tan
than
van
began
caveman
conman
deadpan
dustpan
Japan
kaftan
lifespan
marked man
sandman
suntan
time span
wingspan
also-ran
caravan
frying pan
handyman
highwayman
man-to-man
marzipan
Peter Pan
right-hand man
spick and span
catamaran
flash in the pan
orang-utan
removal van
deliveryman

my gran is a fan of the orang-utan

ance

chance	stance	entrance	tap dance
dance	trance	fat chance	fighting chance
France	advance	folk dance	half a chance
glance	barn dance	freelance	not a chance
lance	break dance	last chance	song and dance
prance	by chance	rain dance	take a chance

ants

chants	plants	enchants	pot plants
grants	slants	house plants	transplants

and

and	by hand	sweatband	overland
band	crash-land	wasteland	promised land
brand	dreamland	waveband	rubber band
gland	expand	withstand	secondhand
grand	forehand	beforehand	sleight of hand
hand	freehand	contraband	underhand
land	grandstand	fairyland	understand
sand	grassland	hand in hand	wonderland
stand	handstand	helping hand	cloud-cuckoo land
strand	headstand	lend a hand	misunderstand
armband	offhand	no man's land	never-never land
backhand	old hand	one man band	
bandstand	quicksand	out of hand	

anned

banned	fanned	planned	spanned
canned	manned	scanned	tanned

We scanned –
Empty shoreline,
Where oystercatchers stand –
Black and white wings flick; thin red beaks
Sift sand.

-ane to -angle

ane

bane, cane, crane, lane, mane, pane, plane, sane, vane, wane, humane, insane, aeroplane, sugar cane, weathervane, windowpane

ain

brain, chain, drain, grain, main, pain, plain, rain, Spain, sprain, stain, strain, train, vain, again, complain, contain, explain, food chain, remain, tearstain, acid rain, down the drain, scatterbrain

ein

rein, vein, chow mein

eign

reign

ang

bang, clang, fang, gang, hang, pang, prang, rang, sang, slang, sprang, tang, twang, chain gang, boomerang, overhang

ingue

meringue

angle

angle, bangle, dangle, jangle, mangle, spangle, strangle, tangle, wrangle, quadrangle, rectangle, triangle, untangle, jingle-jangle

Never let –
Your braces dangle –
When you're standing –
By a mangle!

ank

bank
blank
clank
crank
dank
drank
flank
frank
lank
plank
prank
sank
shrank
spank
stank
swank
tank
thank
yank
fish tank
gangplank
point-blank
sandbank
bottle bank
break the bank
draw a blank
savings bank
walk the plank

ant

ant
pant
rant
scant

antic

antic
frantic
Atlantic
gigantic
pedantic
romantic
transatlantic
unromantic

ap

bap
cap
chap
clap
flap
gap
lap
map
nap
rap
sap
scrap
slap
snap
strap
tap
trap
wrap
yap
zap
cat flap
hubcap
icecap
kidnap
kneecap
last lap
man trap
mishap
mousetrap
nightcap
recap
suntrap
unwrap
watchstrap
baseball cap
booby trap
handicap
overlap
thinking cap
thunderclap

ape

ape
cape
drape
gape
grape
nape
scrape
shape
tape
agape
escape
landscape
red tape
seascape
shipshape
bow and scrape
fire escape
out of shape
narrow escape
videotape

an ape
in a cape

a -arch to -ark

arch

arch, march, March, parch, starch, frogmarch, quick march, on the march

arch	March	starch	quick march
march	parch	frogmarch	on the march

ard

card	yard	graveyard	scorecard
guard	bombard	lifeguard	scrapyard
hard	coastguard	mallard	bodyguard
lard	farmyard	mudguard	credit card
shard	fireguard	postcard	leotard

arred

barred	marred	sparred	tarred
charred	scarred	starred	ill-starred

arf

scarf
headscarf

affe

giraffe

alf

calf	behalf	better half
half	other half	half and half

aph

graph
autograph
paragraph
photograph

augh

laugh
last laugh
belly laugh
hollow laugh

ark

ark	earmark	leap in the dark
bark	embark	safari park
dark	landmark	
hark	postmark	
lark	remark	
mark	skylark	
park	theme park	
shark	double-park	
spark	Noah's ark	
aardvark	question mark	
bookmark	keep in the dark	

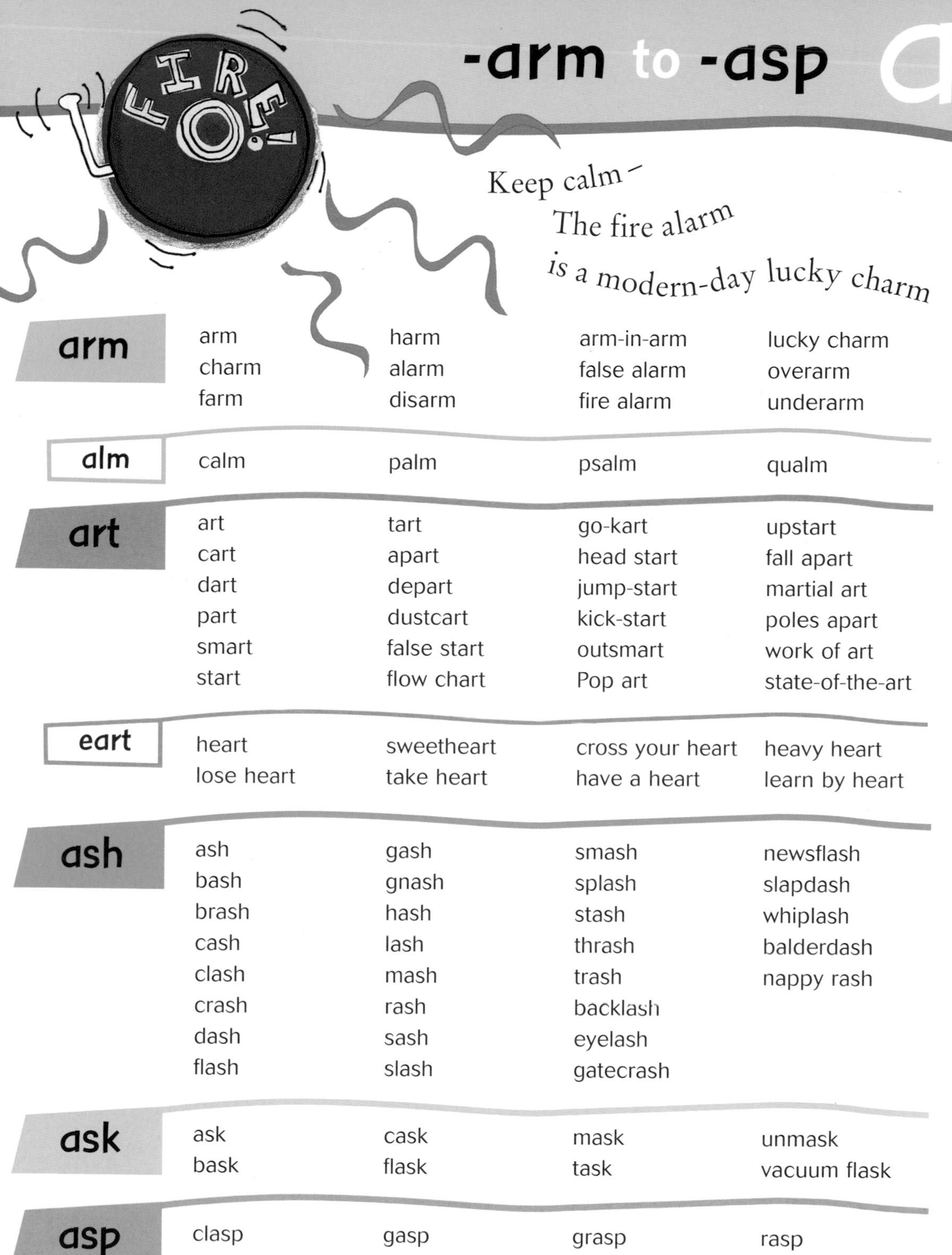

Keep calm –
The fire alarm
is a modern-day lucky charm

arm	arm charm farm	harm alarm disarm	arm-in-arm false alarm fire alarm	lucky charm overarm underarm
alm	calm	palm	psalm	qualm
art	art cart dart part smart start	tart apart depart dustcart false start flow chart	go-kart head start jump-start kick-start outsmart Pop art	upstart fall apart martial art poles apart work of art state-of-the-art
eart	heart lose heart	sweetheart take heart	cross your heart have a heart	heavy heart learn by heart
ash	ash bash brash cash clash crash dash flash	gash gnash hash lash mash rash sash slash	smash splash stash thrash trash backlash eyelash gatecrash	newsflash slapdash whiplash balderdash nappy rash
ask	ask bask	cask flask	mask task	unmask vacuum flask
asp	clasp	gasp	grasp	rasp

a -ass to -atch

ass	brass class glass grass	pass bypass first class outclass	spyglass surpass bold as brass second class	smooth as glass underpass magnifying glass
ast	blast cast fast last mast	past vast aghast at last contrast	downcast forecast full blast half-mast outcast	outlast all-star cast at long last first and last overcast
assed	classed	grassed	passed	surpassed
at	at bat brat cat chat fat flat gnat hat mat pat rat sat	spat splat that vat chitchat combat cowpat dingbat doormat fall flat fat cat hardhat like that	old hat place mat sunhat tomcat top hat wildcat wombat acrobat alley cat babysat copycat cowboy hat habitat	just like that pit-a-pat puppy fat pussycat scaredy cat smell a rat tabby cat this and that tit for tat ziggurat aristocrat blind as a bat rat-a-tat-tat
atch	catch hatch latch match patch scratch	snatch thatch crosspatch knee patch mismatch unlatch	boxing match cabbage patch elbow patch football match met his match mix and match	shooting match slanging match tennis match game, set and match
ach	attach	detach		

ate

ate	frustrate	detonate	roller skate
crate	ice skate	duplicate	second-rate
date	irate	educate	sell-by date
fate	migrate	estimate	separate
gate	playmate	excavate	up to date
grate	primate	fascinate	vaccinate
hate	rotate	germinate	abbreviate
late	schoolmate	hesitate	accelerate
mate	shipmate	hibernate	appreciate
plate	stalemate	illustrate	assassinate
rate	third-rate	imitate	at any rate
skate	translate	incubate	communicate
state	update	indicate	cooperate
blind date	vibrate	insulate	deliberate
cheapskate	calculate	irritate	evaporate
checkmate	celebrate	make a date	exaggerate
create	complicate	meditate	exasperate
cut-rate	concentrate	number plate	interrogate
debate	confiscate	operate	investigate
estate	decorate	out of date	refrigerate
first-rate	demonstrate	overate	reverberate

aight

straight

ait

bait	wait	await	portrait

eight

eight	lightweight	overweight	figure of eight
freight	featherweight	paperweight	
weight	heavyweight	underweight	

ete

fête

Is a lightweight heavyweight
The same as a featherweight?

a -ator to -atty

'Waiter, waiter, there's an alligator
With a calculator in my soup!'
'That adds up!' snapped the waiter.

ator

creator
dictator
equator
narrator
spectator
translator
alligator
calculator
escalator
illustrator
incubator
navigator
operator
radiator
simulator
ventilator

aiter

waiter

aitor

traitor

ater

cater
crater
grater
later
skater
roller skater
see you later
sooner or later

atter

batter
chatter
clatter
fatter
flatter
latter
matter
natter
patter
platter
scatter
shatter
splatter
bespatter
grey matter
pitter-patter
what's the matter?
mad as a hatter
mind over matter
no laughing matter

attle

battle
cattle
rattle
tittle-tattle

atty

batty
catty
chatty
natty
patty
ratty
scatty
tatty

ave			
brave	pave	wave	shockwave
cave	rave	behave	microwave
crave	save	brainwave	misbehave
gave	shave	forgave	rant and rave
grave	slave	heatwave	tidal wave

ay			
bay	way	Monday	break away
bray	archway	no way	break of day
clay	away	okay	by the way
day	betray	one-way	castaway
fray	birthday	pathway	holiday
hay	child's play	railway	market day
lay	decay	runway	Milky Way
may	delay	some day	motorway
pay	doorway	subway	night and day
play	essay	Sunday	runaway
pray	fair play	Thursday	Saturday
ray	Friday	Tuesday	stowaway
say	gangway	today	straightaway
spray	halfway	Wednesday	takeaway
stay	highway	weekday	wedding day
stray	hooray	x-ray	yesterday
sway	horseplay	alleyway	day after day
tray	midday	anyway	red-letter day

é			
café	pâté	fiancé	fiancée

eigh			
neigh	sleigh	weigh	bobsleigh

et			
ballet	bouquet	chalet	sachet
beret	buffet	duvet	ricochet

ey			
grey	prey	obey	disobey
hey	they	survey	

a -aze

aze	blaze	gaze	laze	amaze
	craze	glaze	maze	stargaze
	daze	graze	raze	trailblaze
	faze	haze	ablaze	stony gaze
aise	praise	raise	mayonnaise	
ase	phase	phrase	erase	rephrase
ays	bays	stays	essays	x-rays
	brays	strays	pathways	alleyways
	days	sways	railways	castaways
	frays	trays	runways	gamma rays
	lays	ways	school days	holidays
	pays	always	sideways	market days
	plays	betrays	some days	nowadays
	prays	birthdays	subways	runaways
	rays	delays	Sundays	stowaways
	sprays	doorways	weekdays	good old days

Guess the riddles

Tasty date
Once a year
I come round
adding another candle
to the icing
on your cake ...

Skyline smoker
Sitting
like a hat.
Smoking
like a pipe ...

answers: birthdays chimney

e	be	me	we	excuse me
	he	she	posse	recipe
ea	flea	sea	deep-sea	sweet pea
	pea	tea	high tea	China Sea
	plea	chickpea	North Sea	undersea
ee	bee	wee	settee	guarantee
	fee	agree	sightsee	honeybee
	flee	carefree	tee-hee	jamboree
	free	coffee	teepee	jubilee
	glee	degree	toffee	oversee
	knee	marquee	yippee	pedigree
	see	oak tree	bumblebee	referee
	spree	pine tree	busy bee	refugee
	tee	queen bee	chimpanzee	shopping spree
	three	rupee	Christmas tree	family tree
	tree	set free	disagree	fiddle-de-dee
ey	key	donkey	latchkey	monkey
	chimney	honey	money	valley
i	ski	graffiti	waterski	macaroni
ie	genie	pixie	zombie	walkie-talkie
uay	quay			

Rhyming abbreviations ending in -e sounds

AD	CFC	IT	RIP
BC	DVD	PC	RSVP
CD	ID	PE	VIP

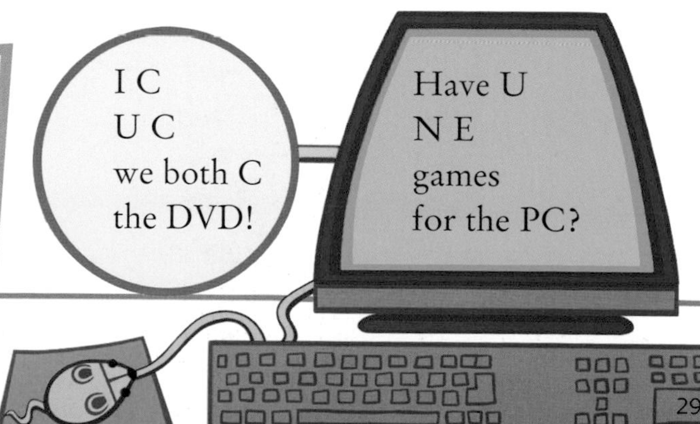

I C
U C
we both C
the DVD!
Have U
N E
games
for the PC?

e -eaf to -eam

eaf	leaf	sheaf	cloverleaf	overleaf
eef	beef	reef	coral reef	roast beef
ief	brief	grief	belief	relief
	chief	thief	big chief	handkerchief
if	motif			
eal	deal	seal	big deal	reveal
	heal	squeal	conceal	unreal
	meal	steal	ideal	wholemeal
	peal	zeal	oatmeal	
	real	appeal	ordeal	
eel	eel	keel	reel	cartwheel
	feel	kneel	steel	freewheel
	heel	peel	wheel	high heel
ile	imbecile	snowmobile	automobile	
eam	beam	steam	ice cream	sunbeam
	cream	stream	mainstream	suncream
	dream	team	moonbeam	upstream
	gleam	bloodstream	off beam	whipped cream
	scream	daydream	pipe dream	in a dream
	seam	downstream	slipstream	let off steam
eem	seem	teem	redeem	self-esteem
eme	scheme	theme	extreme	supreme

Davy Crockett
famous musketeer,
Had three ears –
A left ear, a right ear
And a wild frontier!

ear	clear	rear	hear! hear!	in the clear
	dear	shear	no fear	loud and clear
	ear	smear	unclear	never fear
	fear	spear	pierced ear	overhear
	gear	tear	crystal clear	reappear
	hear	all clear	disappear	
	near	appear	far and near	
eer	beer	peer	career	mountaineer
	cheer	sheer	reindeer	musketeer
	deer	sneer	buccaneer	pioneer
	jeer	steer	engineer	puppeteer
	leer	veer	ginger beer	volunteer
ere	here	revere	atmosphere	insincere
	mere	severe	biosphere	persevere
	sphere	sincere	hemisphere	stratosphere
ier	pier	cashier	cavalier	gondolier
	tier	frontier	chandelier	
ir	souvenir			

e -east to -eat

east

beast
east
feast
least
yeast
at least
beanfeast
northeast
not least
southeast
last but not least

eased

ceased
creased
greased
leased
deceased
decreased
increased
released

iced

policed

ieced

pieced

easy

easy
queasy
uneasy
easy-peasy

eezy

breezy
sneezy
wheezy
lemon squeezy

eat

beat
bleat
cheat
eat
feat
heat
meat
neat
peat
pleat
seat
teat
treat
wheat
backseat
deadbeat
dead heat
defeat
drumbeat
front seat
heartbeat
hot seat
mincemeat
repeat
retreat
overheat
overeat
trick or treat

eet

feet
fleet
greet
meet
sheet
sleet
street
sweet
tweet
backstreet
big feet
cold feet
discreet
groundsheet
flat feet
worksheet
bittersweet
drag your feet
find your feet
itchy feet
parakeet
short and sweet
two left feet

ete

athlete
compete
complete
delete

eater	beater	heater	anteater	fire eater
	eater	neater	eggbeater	two-seater
eetah	cheetah			
eeter	sweeter	teeter		
eter	meter	parking meter		
etre	metre	centimetre	kilometre	millimetre
itre	litre	centilitre	millilitre	
eck	beck	peck	spot-check	risk your neck
	check	speck	bottleneck	smart aleck
	deck	wreck	double check	pain in the neck
	fleck	breakneck	neck and neck	up to your neck
	neck	shipwreck	polo neck	
ech	Czech	high-tech		
ek	trek	pony trek		
eque	cheque	blank cheque	pay cheque	discotheque

Smart Aleck, clever clogs,
Ran a spot-check on his dogs.
Found with ease
– forty fleas!

e -ecks to -ect

ecks			
checks	pecks	shipwrecks	double checks
decks	specks	spot-checks	polo necks
flecks	wrecks	bottlenecks	up to your necks
necks	henpecks	clear the decks	

ex			
flex	vex	index	perplex

ect			
sect	infect	protect	disrespect
collect	inject	reflect	incorrect
connect	insect	reject	self-respect
correct	inspect	respect	sound effect
detect	neglect	select	cause and effect
direct	object	subject	
effect	perfect	suspect	to no effect
eject	prefect	dialect	to good effect
expect	project	disconnect	to take effect

ecked			
checked	pecked	henpecked	spot-checked
flecked	wrecked	shipwrecked	double checked

My uncle Rex
gets henpecked.

His wife says
this is to good effect.

If spot-checked
you can see where the beaks
have left their mark ...

-ed to -edge

My brother said
he'd lost his head –
we found it in
the garden shed!

ed

bed
bled
bred
fed
fled
led
red
shed
shred
sled
sped
wed
airbed
bloodshed
bobsled
bunk bed
deathbed
misled
moped
sickbed
spoonfed
toolshed
well-fed
woodshed
born and bred
bottle fed
feather bed
flowerbed
double bed
garden shed
infrared
newlywed
overfed
quadruped
single bed
underfed

aid

said

ead

bread
dead
dread
head
lead
read
spread
stead
thread
tread
ahead
bedspread
bedstead
behead
big head
blackhead
crispbread
drop dead
egghead
forehead
hothead
instead
outspread
pinhead
redhead
Roundhead
shortbread
skinhead
unthread
well-read
widespread
arrowhead
figurehead
gingerbread
go-ahead
hang your head
keep your head
left for dead
lose your head
overhead
scratch your head
shake your head
sleepyhead
straight ahead
full speed ahead
go to his head
off with her head
over his head

edge

dredge
edge
hedge
ledge
pledge
sledge
wedge
knife edge
on edge
razor's edge

e -eece to -eed

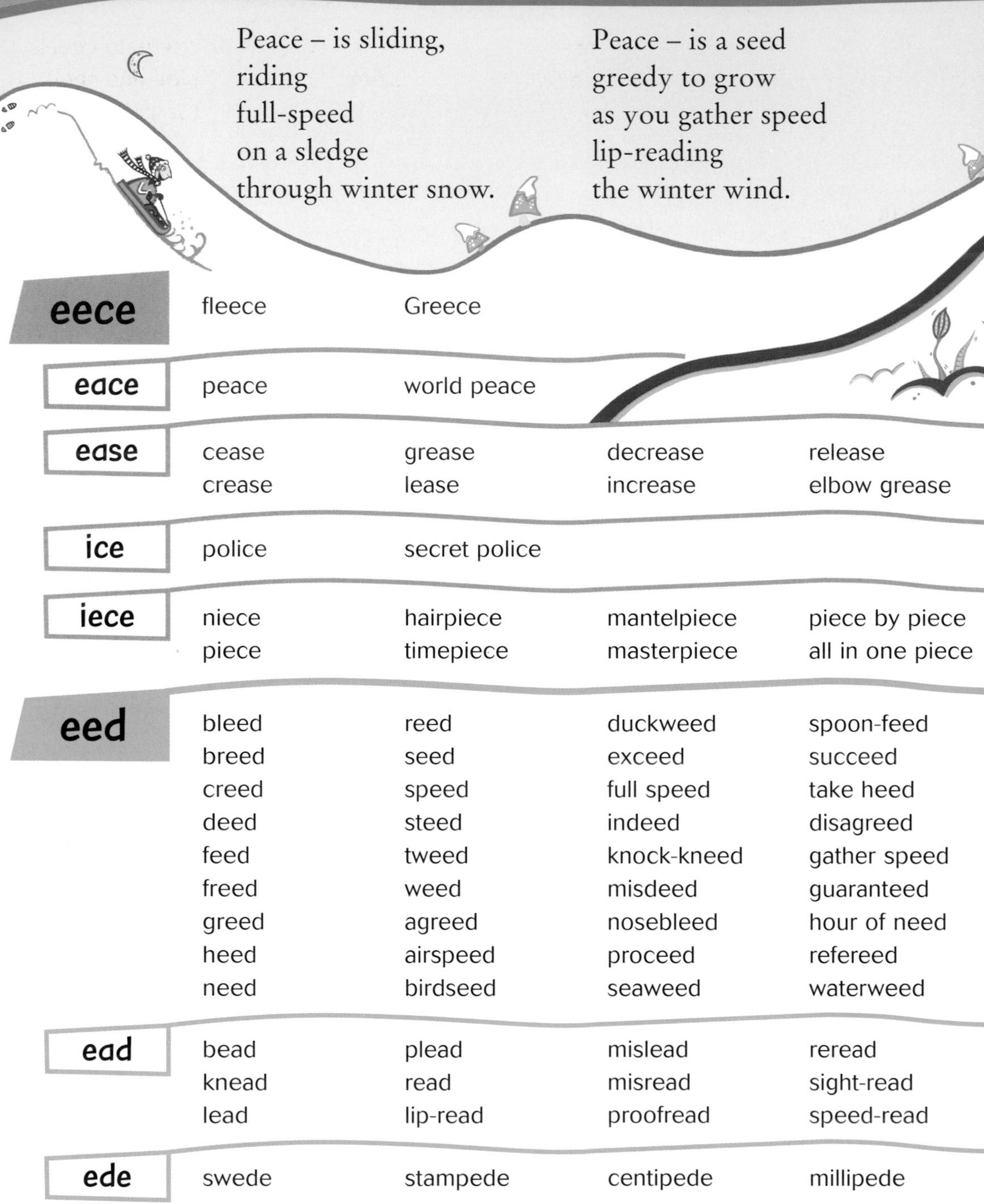

Peace – is sliding,
riding
full-speed
on a sledge
through winter snow.

Peace – is a seed
greedy to grow
as you gather speed
lip-reading
the winter wind.

eece	fleece	Greece		
eace	peace	world peace		
ease	cease crease	grease lease	decrease increase	release elbow grease
ice	police	secret police		
iece	niece piece	hairpiece timepiece	mantelpiece masterpiece	piece by piece all in one piece
eed	bleed breed creed deed feed freed greed heed need	reed seed speed steed tweed weed agreed airspeed birdseed	duckweed exceed full speed indeed knock-kneed misdeed nosebleed proceed seaweed	spoon-feed succeed take heed disagreed gather speed guaranteed hour of need refereed waterweed
ead	bead knead lead	plead read lip-read	mislead misread proofread	reread sight-read speed-read
ede	swede	stampede	centipede	millipede

eek

cheek	leek	seek	cheek-to-cheek
creek	meek	sleek	hide-and-seek
eek!	peek	week	tongue-in-cheek
Greek	reek	midweek	

eak

beak	freak	sneak	tweak
bleak	leak	speak	weak
creak	peak	squeak	so to speak

iek

shriek

ique

clique	boutique	oblique	unique
antique	mystique	technique	fit of pique

een

been	teen	pea-green	evergreen
green	between	sea-green	fairy queen
keen	canteen	sixteen	go-between
preen	eighteen	smokescreen	Hallowe'en
queen	fifteen	sunscreen	movie screen
screen	foreseen	thirteen	multi-screen
seen	fourteen	umpteen	seventeen
sheen	has-been	unseen	sweet sixteen
spleen	nineteen	windscreen	unforeseen

ean

bean	lean	dry-clean	lean and mean
clean	mean	green bean	runner bean
glean	wean	jelly bean	squeaky clean

ene

gene	scene	hygiene	serene

ine

chlorine	routine	limousine	slot machine
cuisine	sardine	magazine	submarine
machine	vaccine	margarine	tambourine
marine	clementine	nectarine	tangerine
ravine	guillotine	quarantine	trampoline

e -eep to -ees

eep	beep bleep cheep creep deep jeep	keep peep seep sheep sleep steep	sweep weep asleep Bo-Peep black sheep knee-deep	skin-deep upkeep ankle-deep beauty sleep chimney sweep oversleep
eap	cheap	heap	leap	reap
ees	bees fees flees frees knees sees sprees trees	agrees decrees degrees marquees rupees sightsees teepees toffees	bumblebees busy bees chimpanzees Christmas trees disagrees dungarees guarantees honeybees	jamborees oversees pedigrees referees refugees shopping sprees the bees' knees
eas	fleas peas	pleas seas	chickpeas high seas	sweet peas overseas
ease	ease	please	tease	disease
eese	cheese	big cheese	say cheese	soft cheese
eize	seize			
ese	these	Chinese	Japanese	Pekinese
eys	keys chimneys	donkeys monkeys		
eze	breeze freeze	sneeze squeeze	wheeze trapeze	unfreeze antifreeze

eg

beg
dreg
egg
keg
leg
peg
bad egg
nutmeg
off the peg
chicken-and-egg
an arm and a leg

ell

bell
cell
dwell
fell
hell
quell
sell
shell
smell
spell
swell
tell
well
yell
bluebell
bombshell
cowbell
doorbell
dumbbell
eggshell
farewell
misspell
nutshell
oil well
retell
seashell
unwell
cockleshell
dinner bell
just as well
magic spell
prison cell
very well
wishing well
alive and well
clear as a bell
not very well
saved by the bell
sound as a bell

el

gel
excel
expel
hotel
lapel
motel
propel
rebel
caramel
carousel
citadel
parallel

ello

cello
hello

ellow

bellow
fellow
mellow
yellow

Bellow 'hello'
to the mellow
yellow fellow
as he plays
on his cello.

elp

help
kelp
whelp
yelp

e -elt to -ench

elt

belt, Celt, dwelt, felt, knelt, melt, pelt, heartfelt, seatbelt, at full pelt, below the belt, under your belt

belt	felt	pelt	at full pelt
Celt	knelt	heartfelt	below the belt
dwelt	melt	seatbelt	under your belt

em

gem	stem	mayhem	Bethlehem
hem	them	modem	

en

den	pen	yen	citizen
fen	ten	amen	felt-tip pen
glen	then	Big Ben	fountain pen
hen	when	pigpen	lion's den
men	wren	playpen	mother hen

The job of Big Ben,
famous London citizen,
Is to tell you when ...

ence

fence	defence	pretence	sit on the fence
pence	offence	self-defence	

ense

dense	expense	incense	sixth sense
sense	good sense	make sense	suspense
tense	immense	nonsense	common sense

ench

bench	drench	quench	trench
clench	French	stench	wrench

-end to -ent e

I tend to drive
my girlfriend
round the bend –
but she catches a bus back!

end

bend
blend
end
friend
lend
mend
send
spend
tend
trend
ascend
attend
backbend
bad end
befriend
best friend
boyfriend
dead end
deep end
defend
depend
descend
extend
girlfriend
intend
Land's End
offend
pen friend
pretend
sharp end
suspend
unbend
upend
wits' end
apprehend
bitter end
end to end
on the mend
overspend
recommend
sticky end
around the bend
at a loose end

ender

blender
fender
gender
lender
sender
slender
tender
big spender
defender
offender
surrender
weekender

ent

bent
cent
dent
lent
rent
scent
sent
spent
tent
vent
went
ascent
cement
consent
content
descent
event
for rent
fragment
invent
lament
per cent
present
prevent
relent
resent
torment
well-spent
big event
came and went
compliment
discontent
heaven sent
main event
ornament
overspent
represent
experiment
happy event
in any event

eant

leant
meant

e -ept to -ess

ept

crept
kept
slept
swept
wept
accept
except
inept
rainswept
windswept
intercept
overslept

epped

stepped
sidestepped
overstepped

erry

berry
cherry
ferry
merry
blackberry
blueberry
gooseberry
make merry
raspberry
strawberry
elderberry

ery

very

ury

bury

esh

flesh
fresh
mesh
thresh
afresh
gooseflesh
refresh
in the flesh

ess

bless
chess
cress
dress
guess
less
mess
press
stress
tress
abcess
access
address
caress
confess
depress
digress
distress
duress
excess
express
headdress
helpless
impress
kindness
lifeless
mattress
nightdress
oppress
possess
princess
progress
repress
success
sundress
undress
unless
fancy dress
loneliness
more or less
new address
nonetheless
second-guess
watercress

es

yes

est

best
chest
crest
guest
jest
lest
nest
pest
quest
rest
test
vest
west
zest
arrest
bequest
conquest
contest
crow's nest
detest
digest
foot-rest
head-rest
infest
invest
next best
northwest
protest
request
southwest
suggest
unrest
Wild West
all the best
do your best
driving test
hornet's nest
last request
level best
past its best
treasure chest
bulletproof vest
under arrest

east

breast
abreast
red-breast

essed

blessed
dressed
guessed
messed
pressed
stressed
addressed
caressed
confessed
depressed
digressed
distressed
expressed
impressed
obsessed
possessed
progressed
undressed
overdressed
unimpressed

In my mind's treasure chest –
Is a hornet's nest of ideas, restlessly buzzing;
Is the contest between the unicorn and the lion,
observed by an unimpressed robin red-breast;
Is a nest of comfort, where the strangest guest rests,
a jester that I call 'Imagination'.

e -et to -eve

et

bet, fret, get, jet, met, net, pet, set, vet

wet, yet, all set, dragnet, duet, filmset, fishnet, forget, get set

handset, headset, jet set, not yet, quartet, quick set, quintet, regret, sunset

Tibet, upset, alphabet, clarinet, dripping wet, Internet, safety net, teacher's pet

eat

sweat, threat

ette

baguette, brunette, cassette, courgette

croquette, launderette, omelette, rosette

roulette, kitchenette, maisonette, pirouette

serviette, silhouette, usherette

etch

fetch, sketch, stretch, wretch

ettle

kettle, mettle, nettle, settle

etal

metal, petal, rose petal, heavy metal

eve

eve, sleeve, Christmas Eve

eave

heave, leave, weave

eive

deceive, perceive, receive

ieve

grieve, achieve

believe, relieve

reprieve, retrieve

disbelieve, make-believe

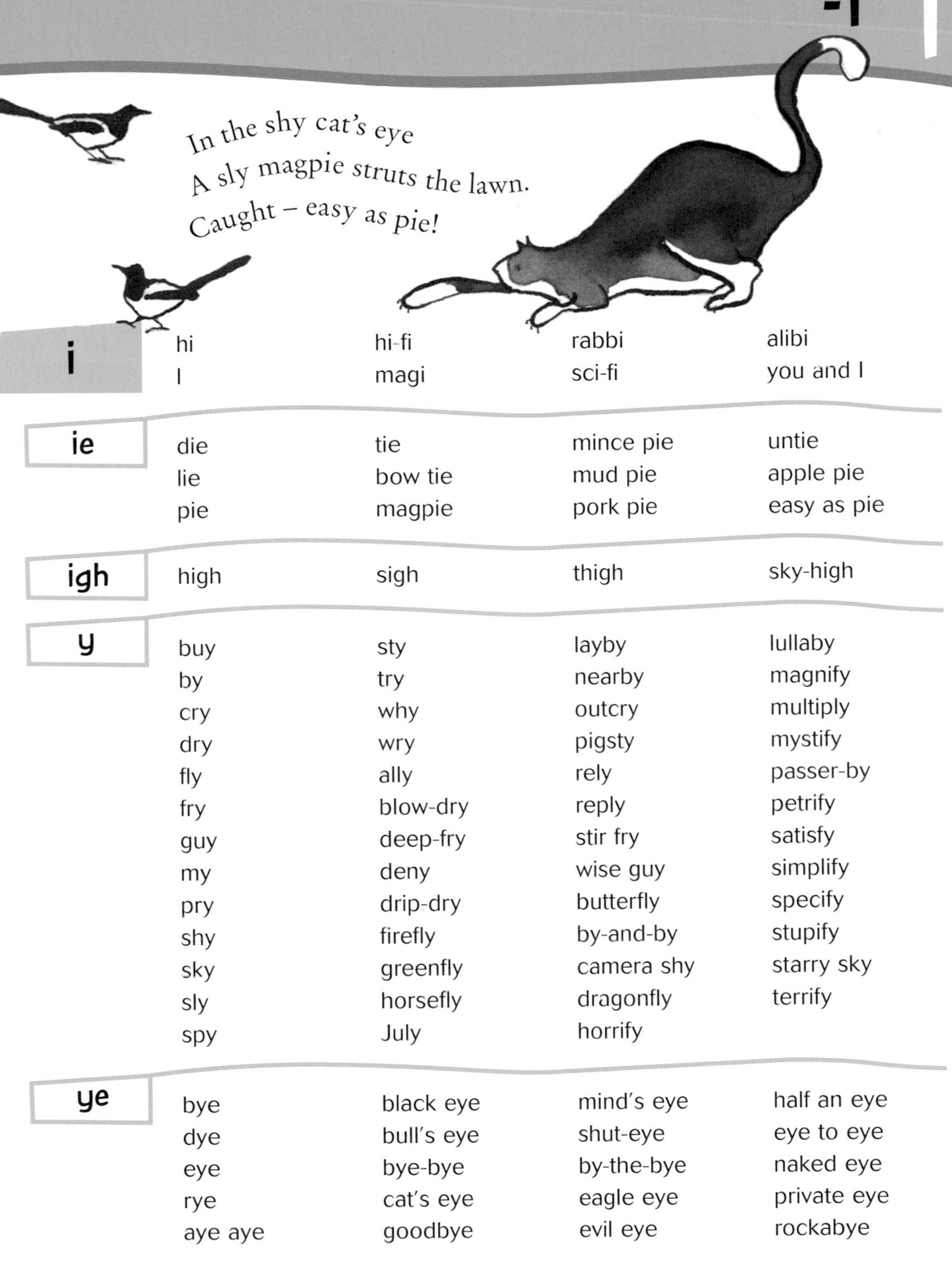
In the shy cat's eye
A sly magpie struts the lawn.
Caught – easy as pie!

i	hi	hi-fi	rabbi	alibi
	I	magi	sci-fi	you and I
ie	die	tie	mince pie	untie
	lie	bow tie	mud pie	apple pie
	pie	magpie	pork pie	easy as pie
igh	high	sigh	thigh	sky-high
y	buy	sty	layby	lullaby
	by	try	nearby	magnify
	cry	why	outcry	multiply
	dry	wry	pigsty	mystify
	fly	ally	rely	passer-by
	fry	blow-dry	reply	petrify
	guy	deep-fry	stir fry	satisfy
	my	deny	wise guy	simplify
	pry	drip-dry	butterfly	specify
	shy	firefly	by-and-by	stupify
	sky	greenfly	camera shy	starry sky
	sly	horsefly	dragonfly	terrify
	spy	July	horrify	
ye	bye	black eye	mind's eye	half an eye
	dye	bull's eye	shut-eye	eye to eye
	eye	bye-bye	by-the-bye	naked eye
	rye	cat's eye	eagle eye	private eye
	aye aye	goodbye	evil eye	rockabye

i -ib to -ick

ib

bib crib fib rib

ibble

dribble nibble quibble scribble

ice

dice	price	trice	half-price
ice	rice	twice	think twice
lice	slice	advice	break the ice
mice	spice	black ice	once or twice
nice	splice	cut-price	sacrifice

ise

concise precise paradise fool's paradise

ick

brick	sick	drumstick	pinprick
chick	slick	gimmick	seasick
click	stick	hat trick	candlestick
flick	thick	homesick	dirty trick
kick	tick	lipstick	double quick
lick	trick	matchstick	limerick
pick	broomstick	nitpick	pogo stick
quick	chopstick	non-stick	walking stick

ic

hic	tactic	mosaic	acrobatic
attic	tragic	organic	automatic
basic	bionic	Pacific	prehistoric
comic	elastic	terrific	supersonic
garlic	electric		
hectic	fantastic		
magic	historic		
music	horrific		
panic	lunatic		
picnic	majestic		
plastic	mechanic		
public	metallic		

icks

bricks
chicks
clicks
flicks
kicks
licks
nicks
picks
pricks
sticks
ticks
tricks
broomsticks
card tricks
chopsticks
drumsticks
for kicks
hand-picks
gimmicks
matchsticks
pinpricks
bag of tricks
candlesticks
dirty tricks
fiddlesticks
pick-up-sticks
ton of bricks
walking sticks

ics

tics
antics
comics
picnics
tropics
aerobics
gymnastics
hysterics

ix

fix
mix
six
cake mix
matrix
phoenix
quick fix
appendix
in a fix
pick and mix
twenty-six
sixty-six

id

bid
did
grid
hid
kid
lid
quid
rid
skid
slid
squid
eyelid
forbid
humid
liquid
livid
rapid
rigid
timid
valid
vivid
whizz kid
invalid
pyramid

iddle

diddle
fiddle
griddle
middle
riddle
twiddle
fit as a fiddle
pig in the
middle

DIY nursery rhyme

Hey diddle diddle, one pig in the middle,
Two mice leapt over the sun,
The little cat purred to see such fun
And the dog flew away with the bun!

-ide

ide	bride	tide	high tide	seaside
	glide	wide	hillside	worldwide
	guide	aside	inside	alongside
	hide	astride	joyride	countryside
	pride	backside	landslide	far and wide
	ride	bedside	low tide	pesticide
	side	decide	offside	riverside
	slide	divide	outside	side by side
	stride	fireside	roadside	slip and slide
ied	cried	spied	relied	multiplied
	died	tied	replied	mystified
	dried	tried	tongue-tied	petrified
	fried	deep-fried	untied	satisfied
	lied	denied	horrified	terrified
ighed	sighed			
yed	eyed	cock-eyed	pop-eyed	eagle-eyed
	bright-eyed	cross-eyed	red-eyed	goggle-eyed

Listen

At the riverside
Listen to the tongue-tied reeds
Whisper in the wind.

At the seaside
listen to the slow *sl*ip and *sl*ide
of the restless tide.

At the roadside
Listen to the goggle-eyed drivers
Tied to the wheel.

At the fireside
Listen to the bright-eyed flame
name the hearth and heart.

idge

bridge, fridge, midge, ridge, squidge, drawbridge, footbridge, porridge

ies

cries, dies, dries, flies, fries, lies, pies, skies, spies, ties, tries, blow-dries, blue skies, bow ties, deep-fries, fireflies, French fries, magpies, mince pies, mud pies, pigsties, pork pies, replies, butterflies, dragonflies, horrifies, lullabies, magnifies, multiplies, petrifies, starry skies, terrifies

ighs

highs, sighs, thighs

ise

guise, prise, rise, wise, advise, arise, clockwise, disguise, high-rise, likewise, sunrise, surprise, unwise, advertise, exercise, televise

ize

prize, size, capsize, first prize, king-size, life-size, outsize, booby prize, hypnotize, idolize, memorize, mesmerize, mobilize, realize, recognize, apologize

ife

knife, life, wife, jackknife, penknife, wildlife, large as life, pocketknife, true to life, husband and wife, not on your life

iff

biff, cliff, sniff, stiff, tiff, whiff, scared stiff, skewwhiff

if

if, as if, what if?

-ift to -iggle

Snowdrift

Overnight
Snow drifts,
And leaves a gift of white.
Twigs wear judge's wigs.

Midnight moonlight
Invites the moon's soft lamplight.

Tonight, starlight speckles the dark.
The wind lifts soft drifts.

Streetlights take the limelight –
Write cold messages in the darkness.

Headlights blare –
A fox freezes, trapped in stage fright,
Takes swift goodnight flight for home.

ift	drift	shift	adrift	shoplift
	gift	sift	face lift	ski lift
	lift	swift	makeshift	snowdrift
	rift	thrift	night shift	spendthrift
iffed	biffed	miffed	sniffed	whiffed
ig	big	jig	twig	oil rig
	dig	pig	wig	guinea pig
	fig	sprig	bigwig	whirligig
	gig	swig	earwig	
iggle	giggle	niggle	wiggle	
	jiggle	squiggle	wriggle	

-ight to -ike

ight

bright
fight
flight
fright
height
knight
light
might
night
plight
right
sight
slight
tight
airtight
all-night
all right
bullfight
daylight
delight
eyesight
firelight
fistfight
flashlight
floodlight
forthright
fortnight
good night
headlight
highlight
insight
lamplight
limelight
midnight
moonlight
outright
oversight
playwright
searchlight
skintight
skylight
spotlight
stage fright
starlight
streetlight
sunlight
tonight
twilight
upright
candlelight
copyright
day or night
dead of night
fly-by-night
out of sight
overnight
pillow fight
second-sight
see the light
watertight
opening night
out like a light
sweetness and light

ite

bite
kite
mite
quite
site
spite
sprite
white
write
fleabite
frostbite
ignite
invite
not quite
polite
recite
snake bite
unite
website
ammonite
appetite
black and white
dynamite
parasite
satellite
stalactite
stalagmite
meteorite

yte

byte
megabyte

ike

bike
hike
like
pike
spike
strike
alike
childlike
dislike
ghostlike
hitchhike
lifelike
snakelike
unlike
warlike
hunger strike
ladylike
look-alike
motorbike
unalike

-ild to -ill

ild	child	mild	wild	godchild
iled	filed	piled	smiled	tiled
ile	file	vile	missile	worthwhile
	mile	while	mobile	crocodile
	Nile	agile	nail file	in a while
	pile	awhile	profile	run a mile
	smile	fragile	reptile	single file
	stile	hostile	turnstile	worth your while
	tile	meanwhile	woodpile	
ial	dial	phial	trial	sundial
isle	aisle	isle		
yle	style	freestyle	hairstyle	lifestyle
ill	bill	kill	till	refill
	brill	mill	trill	sawmill
	chill	pill	will	standstill
	dill	quill	anthill	treadmill
	drill	shrill	downhill	uphill
	fill	sill	fire drill	windmill
	frill	skill	goodwill	overfill
	gill	spill	ill will	overkill
	grill	still	molehill	underfill
	hill	swill	oil spill	windowsill
	ill	thrill	pigswill	over the hill
il	nil	fulfil	until	daffodil
	anvil	tranquil	vigil	

-illy to -im

illy	chilly	hilly	silly-billy	
	frilly	silly	willy-nilly	
illi	chilli			
ily	lily	readily	steadily	
	merrily	Sicily	water lily	
ilt	hilt	kilt	spilt	tilt
	jilt	lilt	stilt	wilt
uilt	built	guilt	quilt	well built
im	brim	prim	swim	minim
	dim	rim	trim	pilgrim
	grim	skim	whim	
	him	slim	denim	
imb	limb			
ym	gym	antonym	pseudonym	synonym
ymn	hymn			

Athletic poem
(say it quickly)

Tim met prim Kim at the gym.
Said Tim to Kim,
'How do you keep such slim limbs Kim?'
'I swim till I'm trim, Tim!' said Kim.

i -ime to -in

ime

chime
crime
dime
grime
lime
mime
prime
slime
time
bedtime
big time
daytime
full-time
half-time
high time
lifetime
meantime
night-time
on time
part-time
pastime
peacetime
playtime
prime time
sometime
springtime
teatime
anytime
behind time
dinnertime
every time
half the time
harvest time
keep in time
one more time
overtime
pantomime
party time
summertime
suppertime
wintertime
all in good time
many a time
not before time
one at a time
time after time
in the nick of time

imb

climb

yme

rhyme
thyme
enzyme
nursery rhyme

in

bin
chin
fin
grin
in
kin
pin
shin
sin
skin
spin
thin
tin
twin
win
bearskin
begin
break-in
cabin
catkin
coffin
dolphin
dustbin
goblin
gremlin
hairpin
javelin
margin
muffin
penguin
puffin
pumpkin
robin
ruin
satin
sequin
sheepskin
stand-in
tailspin
within
double chin
drawing pin
hobgoblin
mandarin
origin
rolling pin
safety pin
terrapin
thick and thin
tigerskin
violin
vitamin

inch	clinch flinch	inch pinch	winch feel the pinch	inch by inch pennypinch
ind	bind blind find grind kind mind	rind wind behind mankind remind rewind	snow-blind unkind unwind bear in mind colourblind humankind	lemon rind mastermind never mind open mind peace of mind spring to mind
igned	signed			
ined	dined lined	pined whined	outlined streamlined	underlined undermined
ine	brine dine fine line mine nine pine shine spine swine twine vine	whine wine airline alpine beeline canine clothesline coastline cloud nine combine divine gold mine	grapevine guideline headline hotline lifeline moonshine outline outshine pipeline punchline shoeshine skyline	sunshine touchline borderline draw the line first in line hold the line porcupine rain or shine rise and shine storyline underline valentine
ign	sign	design	resign	stop sign

Hot Line

i -ing to -ink

ing

bring
cling
fling
king
ping
ring
sing
sling
spring
sting
string
swing
thing
wing

wring
zing
bee sting
boring
building
bullring
ceiling
changeling
clothing
cunning
doing
duckling
earring
farming

fishing
hearing
living
nosering
nothing
pudding
racing
railing
roaring
running
sitting
skating
something
spelling

stunning
whaling
writing
amusing
anything
day-dreaming
diamond ring
everything
exciting
freewheeling
hair-raising
spine-chilling
surprising

inge

binge
cringe

fringe
hinge

singe
tinge

twinge
syringe

ink

blink
brink
chink
clink
drink
ink
kink

link
mink
pink
rink
shrink
sink
slink

stink
think
wink
hoodwink
ice rink
rethink
soft drink

in a wink
let me think
missing link
on the blink
pen and ink
skating rink
tickled pink

inc

zinc

What does this picture poem say?

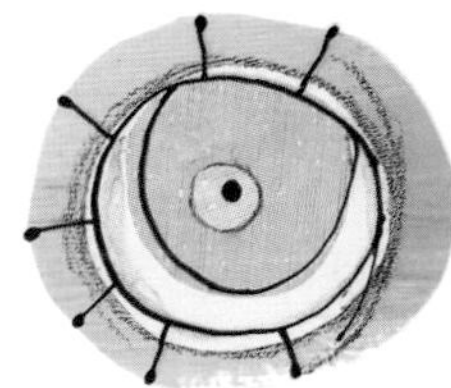

I

think

you

stink!

int

flint	skint	footprint	spearmint
glint	splint	misprint	thumbprint
hint	squint	newsprint	drop a hint
mint	tint	reprint	fingerprint
print	blueprint	skinflint	peppermint

ip

blip	quip	airstrip	comic strip
chip	rip	cowslip	fingertip
clip	ship	field trip	leadership
dip	sip	friendship	lose your grip
drip	skip	gossip	membership
flip	slip	hardship	microchip
grip	snip	non-slip	paperclip
hip	strip	sheep dip	pirate ship
kip	tip	spaceship	championship
lip	trip	tulip	citizenship
nip	whip	warship	premiership
pip	zip	battleship	silicon chip

ipe

gripe	swipe	hornpipe	windpipe
pipe	wipe	peace pipe	guttersnipe
ripe	bagpipe	pinstripe	overripe
stripe	drainpipe	unripe	underripe

ype

hype	type	prototype	stereotype

ire

dire	backfire	empire	perspire
fire	barbed wire	for hire	quagmire
hire	bonfire	gunfire	sapphire
spire	campfire	haywire	vampire
tire	catch fire	inspire	wildfire
wire	desire	on fire	forest fire

yre

tyre	flat tyre

i

-is to -ist

is	his	is	as is	
iz	quiz	showbiz		
izz	fizz	frizz	swizz	whizz
ish	dish fish squish swish	wish brandish goldfish perish	punish rubbish selfish sheepish	shellfish starfish vanish jellyfish
isk	brisk disk	risk whisk	hard disk asterisk	compact disk take a risk
iss	bliss kiss	miss amiss	dismiss near miss	hit or miss give it a miss
ice	malice novice office	practice service accomplice	apprentice cowardice liquorice	precipice self-service secret service
is	this axis	Paris tennis	trellis chrysalis	emphasis portcullis
ist	fist gist list	mist twist wrist	cellist checklist cyclist	insist resist tourist
issed	hissed	kissed	missed	dismissed

it

bit	slit	habit	visit
fit	spit	moonlit	babysit
flit	split	orbit	bit by bit
grit	twit	outfit	every bit
hit	wit	outwit	first-aid kit
it	admit	permit	inhabit
kit	armpit	rabbit	inherit
knit	bandit	smash hit	not a bit
lit	biscuit	summit	perfect fit
nit	bluetit	sunlit	prohibit
pit	circuit	that's it	throw a fit
quit	cockpit	tight fit	banana split
sit	culprit	tool kit	lickety-spit

et

basket	fidget	nugget	rocket
bracelet	gadget	piglet	secret
bucket	helmet	pocket	ticket
carpet	jacket	puppet	triplet
cricket	magnet	racket	trumpet

Moonlit!
Stars are bracelets.
Dark inhabits the park.
Sudden scarlet splits the night sky.
Rocket!

i -itch to -iver

itch	ditch glitch hitch	itch pitch snitch	stitch switch twitch	witch bewitch fever pitch
ich	rich	which	sandwich	ostrich
itter	bitter fitter fritter	glitter knitter litter	sitter skitter twitter	cat litter transmitter babysitter
ive	dive drive five hive I've	jive live alive arrive beehive	high dive high five nose dive revive skydive	survive take five test drive deep sea dive nine to five
iver	liver quiver	river shiver	sliver deliver	downriver upriver

Unidentified Flying Object Rap

The UFO from Mexico –
Didn't give me aggro,
Flew by full of gusto,
Had an eerie halo,
fatter than a hippo,
faster than a rhino,
quicker than a yo-yo,
brighter than a rainbow.

o

go	gusto	pogo	piano
no	halo	rhino	piccolo
so	hello	solo	potato
aggro	hero	UFO	radio
ago	hippo	yo-yo	so-and-so
ammo	info	zero	stereo
banjo	judo	buffalo	studio
bingo	lilo	calypso	to and fro
bongo	logo	commando	tornado
bravo	ludo	flamingo	touch and go
disco	macho	indigo	video
ditto	mango	inferno	volcano
dodo	metro	long ago	yes and no
echo	photo	patio	armadillo

ew

sew

oe

doe	hoe	ice floe	mistletoe
floe	toe	oboe	tale of woe
foe	woe	tiptoe	friend or foe

ough

dough	though	although	even though

ow

blow	slow	good show	shadow
bow	snow	hedgerow	shallow
crow	sow	lie low	sideshow
flow	stow	longbow	sorrow
glow	throw	marrow	window
grow	tow	meadow	bungalow
know	arrow	minnow	ebb and flow
low	below	outgrow	high and low
mow	burrow	pillow	overflow
row	crossbow	rainbow	tomorrow
show	elbow	scarecrow	wheelbarrow

O -oad to -oard

oad

goad	boatload	high road	heavy load
load	by road	ring road	hit the road
road	carload	truckload	on the road
toad	cartload	unload	overload

ode

code	rode	barcode	postcode
ode	strode	explode	episode

owed

crowed	owed	snowed	elbowed
flowed	rowed	stowed	shadowed
glowed	showed	towed	overflowed
mowed	slowed	burrowed	

oard

board	clipboard	outboard	surfboard
hoard	dartboard	scoreboard	whiteboard
aboard	dashboard	skateboard	all aboard
cardboard	floorboard	snowboard	diving board
chessboard	keyboard	springboard	overboard

ard

ward	award	reward	toward

oad

broad	abroad

oared

roared	soared

ord

chord	sword	harpsichord	track record
cord	afford	spinal cord	break the record
fiord	landlord	strike a chord	umbilical cord
lord	record	tape-record	

orde

horde	Concorde

ored

bored	snored	adored	ignored
scored	stored	explored	restored

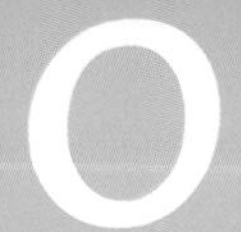

The winter stoat
runs, slim
and quick
as an eel –
its white coat
stained red
from the rabbit's
throat.

oat	boat	throat	sailboat	ferryboat
	coat	afloat	scapegoat	miss the boat
	float	cut-throat	sore throat	motorboat
	gloat	houseboat	speedboat	overcoat
	goat	lifeboat	swingboat	petticoat
	moat	raincoat	waistcoat	powerboat
	stoat	rowboat	billy goat	rock the boat
ote	dote	rote	devote	rewrote
	note	vote	promote	anecdote
	quote	wrote	remote	antidote
ob	blob	lob	sob	hobnob
	bob	mob	throb	odd job
	hob	rob	doorknob	just the job
	job	slob	good job	corn on the cob
	knob	snob	heart-throb	thingamabob
obble	bobble	gobble	hobble	wobble
uabble	squabble			

O -obe to -ocky

obe

globe	robe	earlobe	space probe
probe	strobe	microbe	wardrobe

ock

block	mock	livestock	tick-tock
clock	rock	o'clock	unlock
cock	shock	odd sock	alarm clock
crock	sock	padlock	chock-a-block
dock	stock	peacock	chopping block
flock	airlock	punk rock	cuckoo clock
frock	deadlock	roadblock	hard as rock
knock	gridlock	shamrock	shuttlecock
lock	knock knock	sunblock	weathercock

ocks

blocks	locks	airlocks	peacocks
clocks	mocks	dreadlocks	tick-tocks
docks	rocks	gridlocks	unlocks
flocks	shocks	odd socks	cuckoo clocks
knocks	socks	padlocks	hollyhocks

ox

box	pox	paintbox	paradox
cox	gearbox	postbox	jack-in-the-box
fox	horsebox	toy box	
ox	lunchbox	chatterbox	
	matchbox	chicken pox	

The fat fox with yellow socks
in the horsebox was a chatterbox.

ocky

cocky	rocky	stocky	jabberwocky

ockey

hockey	jockey	disc jockey	ice hockey

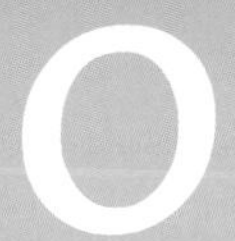

od

clod	plod	shod	tripod
cod	pod	trod	cattle prod
god	prod	hot rod	fishing rod
nod	rod	peapod	

og

bog	grog	backlog	leapfrog
clog	hog	bulldog	road hog
cog	jog	bullfrog	seadog
dog	log	guide dog	ship's log
flog	slog	hedgehog	top dog
fog	smog	hot dog	watchdog
frog	agog	lame dog	underdog

ogue

prologue	catalogue	epilogue	synagogue
analogue	dialogue	monologue	

oil

boil	soil	recoil	aerofoil
broil	spoil	tinfoil	counterfoil
coil	toil	topsoil	hydrofoil
foil	embroil	turmoil	
oil	hard-boil	uncoil	

oyal

loyal	royal	disloyal

oyle

gargoyle

oin

coin	join	adjoin	sirloin
groin	loin	rejoin	flip a coin

oint

joint	gunpoint	viewpoint	prove a point
point	high point	boiling point	score a point
appoint	low point	disappoint	starting point
checkpoint	pinpoint	focal point	beside the point

O -oise to -old

oise	noise	poise	turquoise	traffic noise
oys	boys buoys joys	ploys toys annoys	ballboys cowboys destroys	enjoys killjoys schoolboys
oist	foist	hoist	joist	moist
oke	bloke broke choke joke	poke smoke spoke stroke	woke awoke breaststroke provoke	sunstroke cloud of smoke puff of smoke practical joke
oak	cloak	croak	oak	soak
olk	folk	yolk	old folk	townsfolk
old	bold cold fold gold hold old scold	sold told blindfold catch cold foothold household ice cold	out cold retold scaffold stronghold unfold unsold untold	common cold crock of gold days of old good as gold heart of gold marigold solid gold
oled	soled	cajoled	consoled	paroled
olled	polled rolled	strolled controlled	enrolled patrolled	steamrolled unrolled
ould	mould			

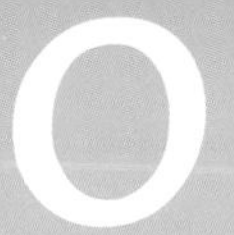

The goldfish speaks

My memory lasts seven seconds –
just long enough to patrol the bowl,
arriving back where I began,
not recognizing where I am;
trapped in a never-ending loophole.

ole	dole hole mole pole role sole stole vole whole	armhole bargepole beanpole black hole cajole console flagpole insole keyhole	loophole manhole maypole North Pole peephole pinhole porthole pothole South Pole	tadpole as a whole buttonhole casserole cubbyhole on the whole rigmarole starring role totem pole
oal	foal	goal	shoal	charcoal
ol	control	patrol	self-control	remote control
oll	roll scroll	stroll drum roll	steamroll unroll	rock and roll
oul	soul	bare your soul	life and soul	body and soul
owl	bowl	fast bowl	fishbowl	sugarbowl
olt	bolt colt	jolt volt	revolt unbolt	thunderbolt

O -ome to -on

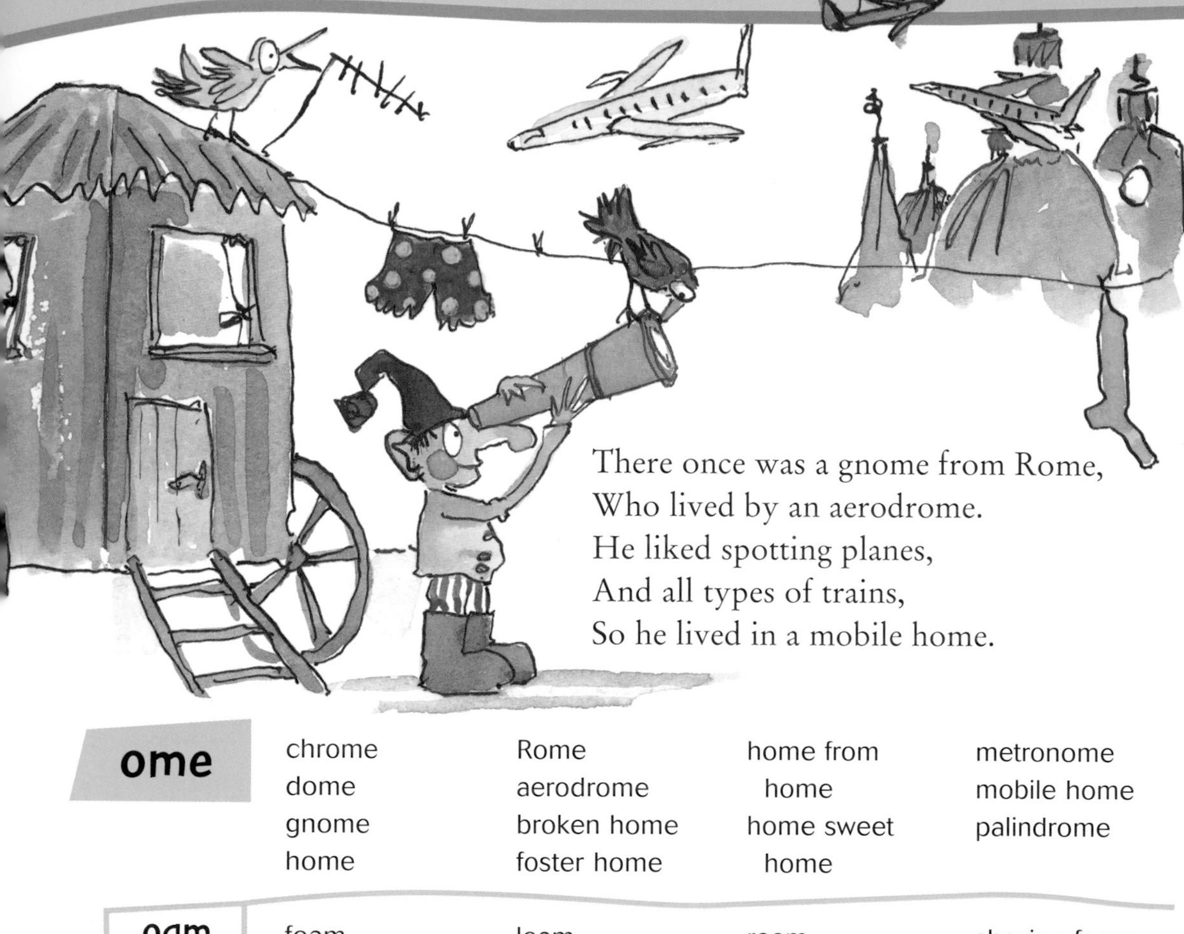

There once was a gnome from Rome,
Who lived by an aerodrome.
He liked spotting planes,
And all types of trains,
So he lived in a mobile home.

ome	chrome dome gnome home	Rome aerodrome broken home foster home	home from home home sweet home	metronome mobile home palindrome
oam	foam	loam	roam	shaving foam
omb	comb	currycomb	honeycomb	
on	con don on anon	baton coupon hands-on icon	neon neutron nylon pylon	salon upon electron off and on
an	swan	wan		
one	gone	scone	shone	all gone

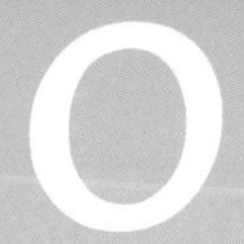

ond	blond bond	fond pond	beyond fishpond	respond vagabond
and	wand	magic wand		
onned	conned	donned		
one	bone clone cone drone lone phone prone scone stone throne tone zone	alone backbone cheekbone fishbone hailstone jawbone kerbstone ozone pine cone postpone shinbone thighbone	time zone tombstone trombone war zone wishbone anklebone cobblestone collarbone funny bone heart of stone ice-cream cone megaphone	microphone mobile phone parking zone rolling stone saxophone skin and bone stepping-stone telephone traffic cone xylophone accident-prone dry as a bone
ewn	sewn	hand-sewn		
oan	groan	loan	moan	moan and groan
own	blown flown grown	mown own shown	sown thrown full-grown	unknown well-known overgrown
ong	bong dong gong long pong prong song	strong throng wrong along belong ding-dong folk song	headlong headstrong Hong Kong love song oblong ping-pong pop song	sarong sing-song so long all along before long in the wrong right or wrong

O -oo

oo	boo coo goo loo moo shoo too	woo zoo a-choo bamboo boo-hoo cuckoo igloo	kazoo shampoo skidoo tattoo voodoo yoo-hoo cockatoo	kangaroo peekaboo didgeridoo hullaballoo tu-whit tu-whoo cock-a-doodle doo
ew	blew brew chew crew dew drew few flew grew	knew mew new pew phew screw shrew slew skew	stew threw view askew brand-new corkscrew nephew on view renew	review sinew unscrew bird's eye view book review interview Irish stew point of view quite a few
ewe	ewe			
o	do to two who	ado hairdo how-to lean-to	says who? to-do undo who's who	two by two well to do how do you do? what a to-do
oe	shoe	canoe	horseshoe	snowshoe
ou	you	thank you	after you	caribou
ough	through all through breakthrough	see through through and through		
ous	rendezvous			

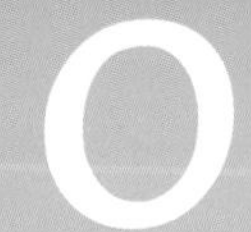

u	flu	guru	kung fu	Peru
	gnu	Hindu	menu	tutu

ue	blue	sue	statue	continue
	clue	true	subdue	navy blue
	cue	argue	tissue	overdue
	due	fondue	unglue	residue
	flue	pursue	untrue	bolt from the blue
	glue	on cue	value	
	hue	rescue	venue	out of the blue
	queue	revue	avenue	red, white and blue
	rue	sky-blue	barbecue	

Barbecue on the ark

The animals came in two by two,
They all queued up for the barbecue –

'Oh, after you,'
said the caribou!

'How do you do,'
said the elder ewe,

'I've a bird's eye view,'
said the cockatoo,

'What a hullaballoo,'
said the kangaroo,

But the old gnu,
as he joined the queue,
said, 'If one gnu is a gnu
then two gnus makes news.'

So he and his wife played
the didgeridoo
while the burgers sizzled
on the barbecue …

O -ood to -ool

ood	good	falsehood	withstood	motherhood
	hood	firewood	babyhood	neighbourhood
	stood	for good	brotherhood	sisterhood
	wood	knighthood	fatherhood	understood
	boyhood	make good	Hollywood	misunderstood
	childhood	plywood	knock on wood	so far so good
	driftwood	touch wood	livelihood	up to no good
ould	could	should	would	
ook	book	rook	notebook	dirty look
	brook	shook	outlook	off the hook
	cook	took	scrapbook	overcook
	crook	cookbook	sketchbook	overlook
	hook	fish hook	songbook	overtook
	look	handbook	textbook	second look
	nook	mistook	comic book	storybook
ool	cool	spool	toadstool	lose your cool
	drool	stool	whirlpool	play it cool
	fool	tool	act the fool	Sunday school
	pool	footstool	April fool	supercool
	school	playschool	boarding school	swimming pool
oul	ghoul			
uel	fuel	refuel		
ule	mule	capsule	as a rule	molecule
	rule	globule	golden rule	overrule
	yule	schedule	minuscule	ridicule

-oom to -oon

oom

bloom	vroom	dark room	bride and groom
boom	zoom	heirloom	dining room
broom	ballroom	houseroom	elbow room
doom	bathroom	mushroom	gloom and doom
gloom	bedroom	playroom	living room
groom	bridegroom	storeroom	sonic boom
loom	classroom	strongroom	
room	cloakroom	tearoom	

ume

fume	plume	costume	perfume

oon

croon	buffoon	new moon	honeymoon
moon	cartoon	platoon	macaroon
noon	cocoon	raccoon	pretty soon
soon	festoon	teaspoon	tablespoon
spoon	full moon	too soon	wooden spoon
swoon	harpoon	twelve noon	hot-air balloon
baboon	lagoon	tycoon	man in the moon
balloon	maroon	typhoon	over the moon
bassoon	monsoon	afternoon	

une

dune	fortune
June	Neptune
prune	sand dune
tune	out of tune

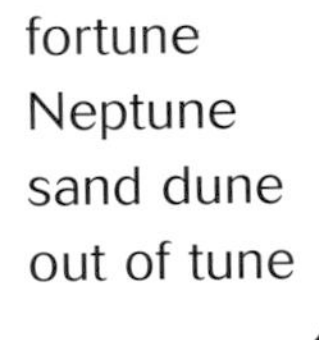

The honeymoon

The raccoon and baboon
left the wedding at noon.
They dined on prunes
and macaroons
by the golden light
of the honey moon.

O -oop to -oot

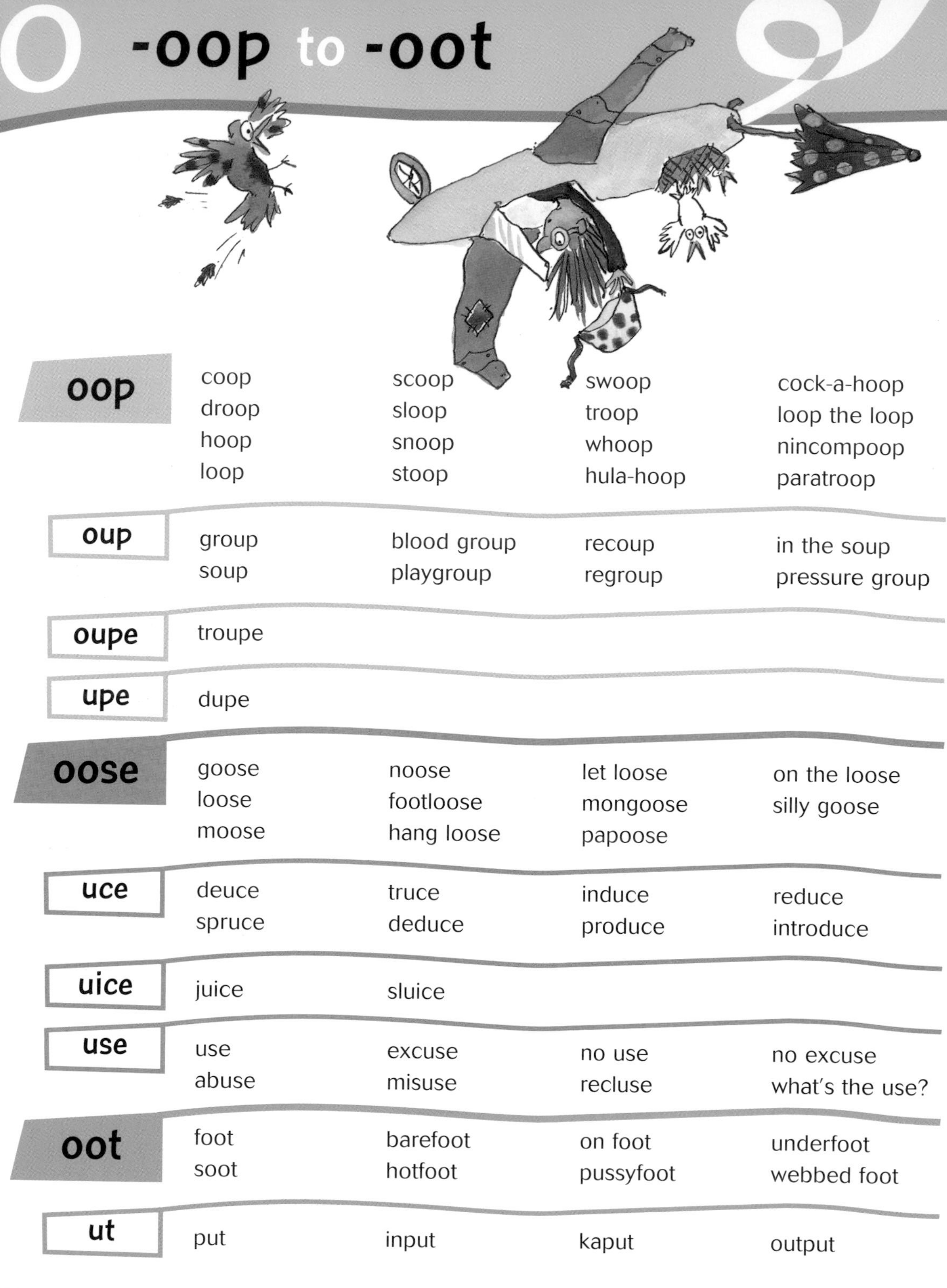

oop	coop droop hoop loop	scoop sloop snoop stoop	swoop troop whoop hula-hoop	cock-a-hoop loop the loop nincompoop paratroop
oup	group soup	blood group playgroup	recoup regroup	in the soup pressure group
oupe	troupe			
upe	dupe			
oose	goose loose moose	noose footloose hang loose	let loose mongoose papoose	on the loose silly goose
uce	deuce spruce	truce deduce	induce produce	reduce introduce
uice	juice	sluice		
use	use abuse	excuse misuse	no use recluse	no excuse what's the use?
oot	foot soot	barefoot hotfoot	on foot pussyfoot	underfoot webbed foot
ut	put	input	kaput	output

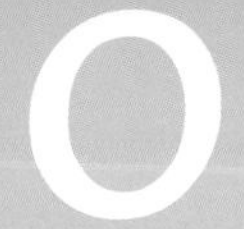

op

bop	prop	hilltop	tip top
chop	shop	hip hop	treetop
cop	slop	lap top	workshop
crop	stop	nonstop	bellyflop
drop	top	pit stop	lollipop
flop	big top	raindrop	mountain top
hop	bookshop	rooftop	set up shop
lop	bus stop	snowdrop	shut up shop
mop	clip-clop	sweetshop	turboprop
plop	eavesdrop	teardrop	window shop
pop	flip-flop	teashop	over the top

ope

cope	rope	antelope	periscope
grope	scope	envelope	skipping rope
hope	slope	gyroscope	stethoscope
lope	elope	horoscope	telescope
mope	tightrope	microscope	kaleidoscope
pope	towrope	not a hope	slippery slope

oap

soap

bar of soap

Fame

Could you cope –
high up, on the tightrope of fame?

Or would it be
that you'd have no hope –
blinded by your name in lights,
lost on your own slippery slope?

O -ore

ore	bore chore core gore lore more ore pore score	shore snore sore store swore tore wore adore ashore	before encore explore eyesore folklore footsore galore ignore no more	seashore therefore all ashore carnivore evermore herbivore nevermore sycamore forevermore
ar	war	all-out war	man-of-war	tug of war
aur	centaur	dinosaur	Minotaur	pterosaur
aw	caw claw draw flaw gnaw jaw law	paw raw saw squaw straw thaw chainsaw	coleslaw guffaw hacksaw jackdaw jigsaw last straw macaw	outlaw pawpaw rubbed raw seesaw luck of the draw quick on the draw
oar	boar oar	roar soar	uproar	
oor	door floor poor	back door front door indoor	next-door outdoor trapdoor	at death's door door-to-door rich or poor
or	for nor	condor mentor	corridor matador	metaphor meteor
our	four	pour	downpour	troubadour

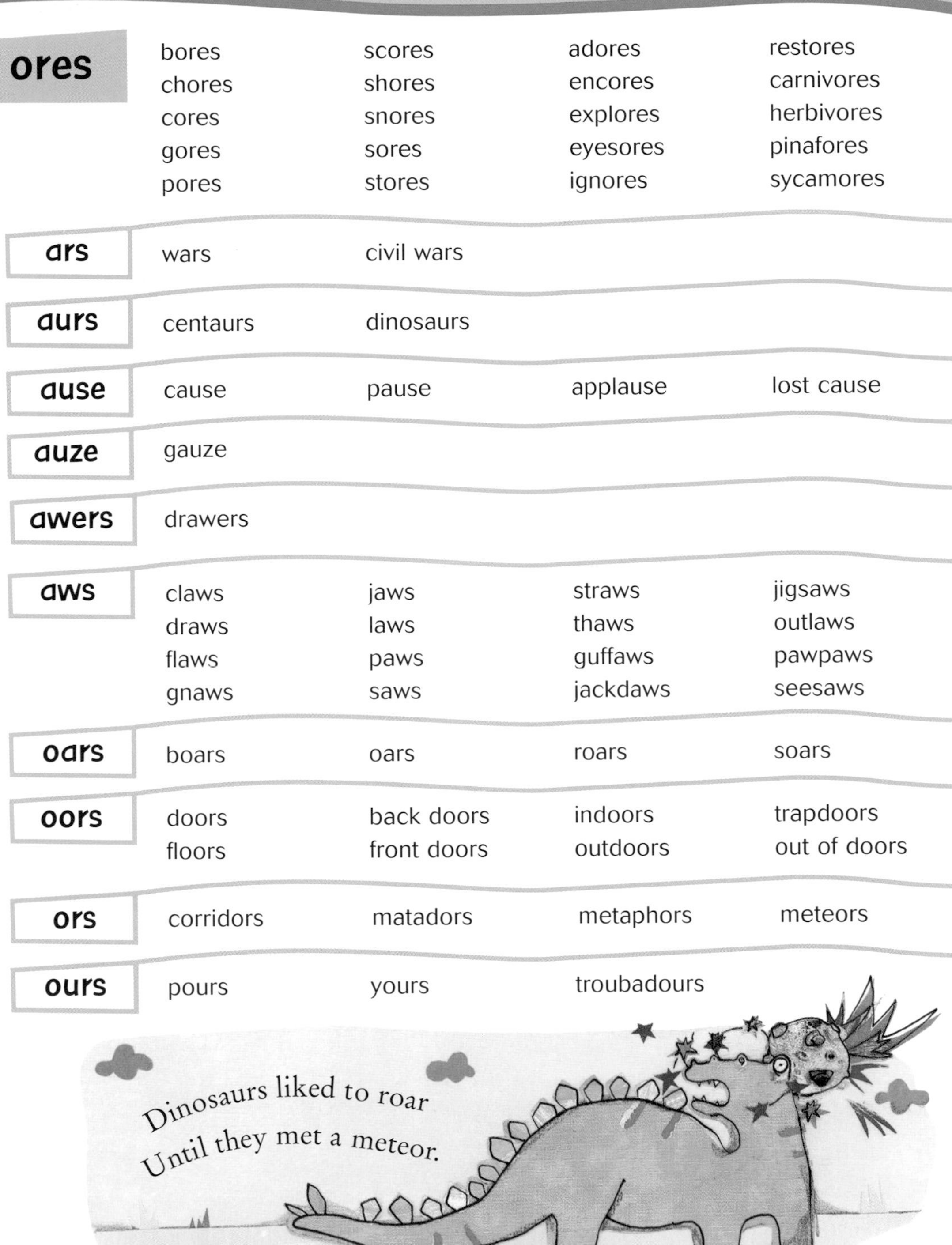

ores	bores chores cores gores pores	scores shores snores sores stores	adores encores explores eyesores ignores	restores carnivores herbivores pinafores sycamores
ars	wars	civil wars		
aurs	centaurs	dinosaurs		
ause	cause	pause	applause	lost cause
auze	gauze			
awers	drawers			
aws	claws draws flaws gnaws	jaws laws paws saws	straws thaws guffaws jackdaws	jigsaws outlaws pawpaws seesaws
oars	boars	oars	roars	soars
oors	doors floors	back doors front doors	indoors outdoors	trapdoors out of doors
ors	corridors	matadors	metaphors	meteors
ours	pours	yours	troubadours	

Dinosaurs liked to roar
Until they met a meteor.

O -ork to -orn

ork	cork fork	pork stork	hayfork New York	pitchfork knife and fork
alk	chalk stalk talk	walk beanstalk catwalk	pep talk sleepwalk small talk	spacewalk sweet talk baby talk
awk	gawk	hawk	squawk	tomahawk
orm	form storm brainstorm	hailstorm inform perform	platform rainstorm sandstorm	snowstorm thunderstorm uniform
arm	swarm	warm	lukewarm	
orn	born corn horn morn scorn shorn	sworn thorn torn worn acorn adorn	first-born foghorn forlorn French horn hawthorn newborn	popcorn sweetcorn well-worn Capricorn peppercorn unicorn
aun	faun	leprechaun		
awn	dawn drawn	lawn pawn	prawn sawn	yawn frogspawn
orne	borne	airborne	seaborne	waterborne
ourn	mourn			

Look out of your window at dawn.
There's a hoofprint, there on the lawn,
A silver hair, caught on a thorn –
You dreamt last night of a unicorn.

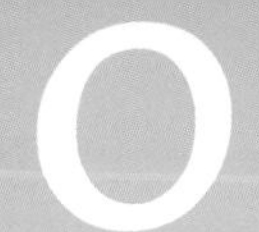

orse	horse Norse carthorse	clothes horse dark horse racehorse	remorse seahorse hobbyhorse	rocking horse Trojan horse eat like a horse
auce	sauce	chocolate sauce		
oarse	coarse	hoarse		
orce	force	by force	divorce	reinforce
ourse	course concourse crash course	golf course main course of course	off course on course racecourse	in due course collision course obstacle course
ort	fort port short snort sort	sport airport bad sport export good sport	passport report resort seaport spoilsport	support transport heliport hold the fort last resort
art	thwart	wart		
aught	caught fraught	taught distraught	onslaught self-taught	
aut	taut	astronaut	juggernaut	
ought	bought brought fought	nought ought thought	close-fought dreadnought afterthought	come to nought deep in thought food for thought
ourt	court	forecourt	law court	tennis court

O -ose to -ost

ose	close	dose	morose	overdose
osh	gosh	nosh	posh	slosh
ash	quash squash	wash brainwash	carwash mouthwash	whitewash
oss	boss cross floss	gloss moss toss	across criss-cross albatross	candyfloss doublecross motocross
ost	ghost host most post	almost bedpost gatepost goalpost	lamppost outpost signpost utmost	innermost outermost perfect host deaf as a post
oast	boast	coast	roast	toast

Deaf as a post,
Grandad always said 'yes'.
A most agreeable host –
I keep his memory
warm as toast.

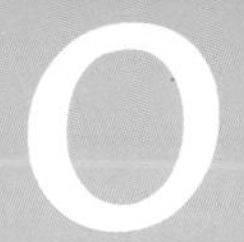

ot	blot	snot	high spot	apricot
	clot	spot	jackpot	beauty spot
	cot	swot	long shot	boiling hot
	dot	tot	mascot	Camelot
	got	trot	mugshot	chimneypot
	hot	big shot	red-hot	coffeepot
	jot	black spot	robot	flowerpot
	knot	blind spot	slip knot	go to pot
	lot	bloodshot	snapshot	hit the spot
	not	cannot	soft spot	in a spot
	plot	crackpot	sunspot	like a shot
	pot	dovecot	teapot	melting pot
	rot	earshot	tight spot	on the dot
	Scot	forgot	topknot	on the spot
	shot	fusspot	upshot	thanks a lot
	slot	gunshot	white hot	forget-me-not
acht	yacht			
at	squat	what	somewhat	what's what
	swat	kumquat	so what?	
otion	lotion	notion	commotion	slow motion
	motion	potion	devotion	magic potion
ocean	ocean			
otty	dotty	knotty	potty	spotty
ouch	couch	grouch	pouch	vouch
	crouch	ouch!	slouch	

O -oud to -ount

oud

cloud
loud
proud
shroud
aloud
out loud
rain cloud
thundercloud

owd

crowd
in crowd
overcrowd
follow the crowd

owed

bowed
cowed
rowed
vowed
wowed
allowed
bow-wowed
meowed

ound

bound
found
ground
hound
pound
round
sound
wound
aground
around
astound
background
bloodhound
dumbfound
earthbound
eastbound
fairground
foreground
foxhound
greyhound
housebound
icebound
newfound
northbound
playground
profound
southbound
spellbound
sports ground
surround
unsound
westbound
year-round
all around
homeward bound
lost and found
outward bound
round and round
solid ground
turnaround
underground
merry-go-round

owned

browned
clowned
crowned
downed
drowned
frowned
gowned
renowned

ount

count
mount
account
amount
discount
head count
keep count
lose count
recount
on no account
out for the count

I can't keep count of this amount,
I'll have to recount.

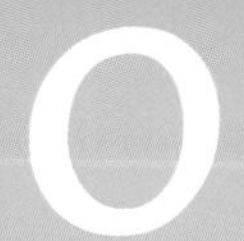

Don't grouse
at the woodlouse,
as it humps
and bumps
its armour-plated house.

ouse

douse	church mouse	keep house	cat and mouse
grouse	doghouse	lighthouse	haunted house
house	dormouse	madhouse	house to house
louse	hothouse	warehouse	summer house

out

bout	trout	knockout	do without
clout	about	lookout	down and out
lout	back out	lose out	hang about
out	blackout	pass out	in and out
pout	breakout	shootout	inside out
scout	check out	sold out	odd man out
shout	chill out	throughout	roundabout
snout	dropout	walk out	on the lookout
spout	hang out	without	over and out
sprout	hideout	workout	up and about

oubt

doubt	in doubt	no doubt	without a doubt

ought

drought

ow

bow	pow	bow-wow	somehow
brow	prow	eyebrow	anyhow
cow	row	for now	here and now
dhow	sow	know-how	solemn vow
how	vow	meow	take a bow
now	wow	now, now	any day now
ow!	allow	pow-wow	any old how

ough

bough	plough	snowplough

O -ower to -own

ower

cowered
flower
glower
power
shower
tower
cornflower
horsepower
manpower
Mayflower
rain shower
sunflower
wallflower
watchtower
wildflower
willpower
cauliflower
overpower
water power
ivory tower

our

flour
hour
our
scour
sour
devour
lunch hour
rush hour
dinner hour
hour by hour
on the hour
sweet and sour

owl

fowl
growl
howl
owl
prowl
scowl
yowl
brown owl
night owl
wildfowl
on the prowl
wise old owl

oul

foul

owel

bowel
towel
trowel
vowel

own

brown
clown
crown
down
drown
frown
gown
town
ballgown
breakdown
comedown
countdown
crackdown
face-down
ghost town
home town
knockdown
letdown
lowdown
meltdown
nightgown
put-down
run-down
showdown
slowdown
splashdown
sundown
touchdown
broken-down
eiderdown
hand-me-down
shantytown
tumble-down
up and down
upside-down
wedding gown

oun

noun

Have you heard the upside-down bird?
Poor night owl, when out on the prowl,
you'll hear it
twoo-twit!

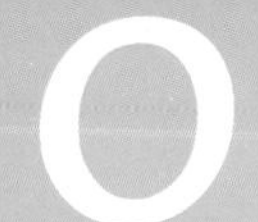

ows

blows	rows	bellows	rainbows
bows	shows	burrows	scarecrows
crows	slows	crossbows	shadows
flows	snows	elbows	sideshows
glows	sows	furrows	bungalows
grows	stows	hedgerows	come to blows
knows	throws	longbows	ebbs and flows
lows	tows	meadows	overflows
mows	arrows	outgrows	overthrows

oes

foes	throes	here goes!	buffaloes
goes	toes	oboes	dominoes
hoes	woes	tiptoes	volcanoes

os

banjos	pianos
bongos	radios
broncos	rodeos
hippos	so-and-sos
ponchos	stereos
rhinos	studios
yo-yos	UFOs
calypsos	videos
dynamos	
flamingos	

ose

chose	those	suppose	look down your nose
close	enclose	wild rose	open and close
hose	expose	decompose	overexpose
nose	fire hose	hold your nose	under your nose
pose	oppose	nose to nose	
prose	primrose	runny nose	
rose	propose	follow your nose	

oze

doze	froze	bulldoze	unfroze

O -oy

oy

boy
buoy
coy
joy
ploy
toy
ahoy
alloy
annoy
ballboy
choirboy
convoy
cowboy
decoy
destroy
employ
enjoy
lifebuoy
playboy
schoolboy
tomboy
corduroy
paperboy
pride and joy

The Shadow

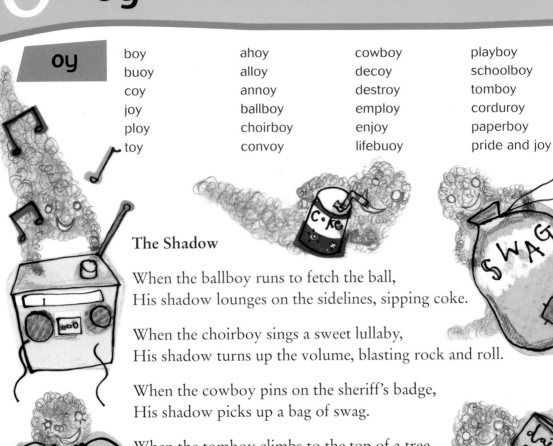

When the ballboy runs to fetch the ball,
His shadow lounges on the sidelines, sipping coke.

When the choirboy sings a sweet lullaby,
His shadow turns up the volume, blasting rock and roll.

When the cowboy pins on the sheriff's badge,
His shadow picks up a bag of swag.

When the tomboy climbs to the top of a tree,
Her shadow puts on a pink, frilly dress.

When the paperboy delivers the daily news,
His shadow chucks the papers into a puddle.

When the lifebuoy saves another life,
The shadow drowns itself …

ub

club	rub	tub	fox cub
cub	scrub	bathtub	hubbub
grub	shrub	bear cub	join the club
hub	snub	cherub	lion cub
pub	stub	fan club	rub-a-dub-dub

ubble

bubble	rubble	stubble	hubble-bubble

ouble

double	deep trouble	at the double	toil and trouble
trouble	see double	double trouble	

uch

much	not much	a bit much	such and such
such	too much	pretty much	not up to much

ouch

touch	lose touch	get in touch	lose your touch
in touch	soft touch	keep in touch	out of touch

utch

clutch	crutch	Dutch	hutch

uck

buck	good luck	thunderstruck
chuck	hard luck	try your luck
cluck	moonstruck	
duck	pot luck	
luck	stagestruck	
muck	unstuck	
pluck	with luck	
puck	worse luck	
struck	horror-struck	
stuck	forklift truck	
suck	no such luck	
truck	panic-struck	
tuck	pass the buck	
yuck	push your luck	
dumbstruck	sitting duck	

U -uckle to -ude

uckle	buckle chuckle	knuckle suckle	belt buckle swashbuckle	honeysuckle
ud	bud dud mud scud	spud stud thud nose stud	rosebud soap sud tastebud chew the cud	clear as mud stick-in-the-mud
ood	blood flood bad blood	blue blood cold blood flash flood	lifeblood sweat blood chill your blood	flesh and blood in your blood
uddle	cuddle	huddle	muddle	puddle
ude	crude nude rude	exclude include intrude	altitude attitude gratitude	latitude longitude solitude
ewed	brewed chewed	mewed screwed	stewed viewed	renewed interviewed
ood	food mood bad mood	dog food fast food foul mood	good mood seafood soul food	baby food in a mood in the mood
ooed	booed cooed	mooed shooed	wooed boo-hooed	shampooed tattooed
ued	cued glued	sued argued	pursued rescued	valued barbecued

udge	budge drudge fudge	grudge judge nudge	sludge smudge trudge	begrudge hot fudge misjudge
uff	bluff buff cuff duff fluff	gruff huff puff scruff scuff	snuff stuff dandruff earmuff handcuff	blindman's buff fisticuff huff and puff overstuff powder puff
ough	rough tough	enough that's tough	fair enough sure enough	enough's enough
ug	bug chug drug dug glug hug	jug lug mug plug rug shrug	slug smug snug thug tug bear hug	bedbug earplug humbug litterbug spark plug unplug

Doug drives a digger.
Don't snigger,
don't shrug,
don't call Doug an ugly mug.
He's no smug thug –
say what you want,
he'll just shrug.
You won't see
a **bigger** figure
than Doug, on his digger.

U -ul to -umb

ul

armful	graceful	restful	watchful
boastful	handful	roomful	wishful
careful	harmful	sackful	beautiful
cheerful	helpful	shameful	colourful
cupful	hopeful	skilful	pitiful
doubtful	hurtful	spoonful	plentiful
dreadful	mouthful	tearful	powerful
faithful	peaceful	useful	sorrowful
fearful	playful	wakeful	wonderful

ool

wool	lambswool	steel wool	cotton wool

ull

bull	pull	cramfull	push-pull
full	chock-full	half-full	overfull

um

chum	scum	plectrum	medium
drum	slum	spectrum	minimum
glum	strum	steel drum	museum
gum	sum	tantrum	pendulum
hum	swum	yum-yum	stadium
mum	tum	asylum	chrysanthemum
plum	album	chewing gum	fee fie fo fum
rum	eardrum	kettle drum	millennium
scrum	humdrum	maximum	

om

freedom	kingdom	stardom	wisdom

ome

come	gruesome	threesome	meddlesome
some	how come?	twosome	overcome
become	outcome	welcome	troublesome

umb

crumb	numb	thumb	Tom Thumb
dumb	plumb	succumb	deaf and dumb

umble	crumble fumble grumble	humble jumble mumble	rumble stumble tumble	apple crumble rough and tumble
ummy	crummy	dummy	mummy	tummy
ump	bump clump dump frump hump jump	lump plump pump rump slump stump	thump trump goosebump high jump long jump ski jump	speed bump tree stump bungee jump rubbish dump running jump sugar lump

The **G**ruesome twosome
Met the awes**O**me foursome,
On the way to the rubbish dump.
The two**S**ome blew some bubble gum
Which made **E**verybody jump.
The **B**last was quite dramatic,
It tore the **U**niverse in two.
But their **M**emory lingers on
In the sha**P**e of an airborne shoe!

U -un to -ung

un	bun fun gun nun pun	run shun spun stun sun	begun dry run for fun shotgun what fun!	hit-and-run jump the gun machine gun on the run trial run
on	son ton	won godson	grandson stepson	stetson
one	done none one all done	no one outdone someone undone	well done all in one all or none anyone	everyone number one one by one over and done
unch	brunch bunch	crunch hunch	lunch munch	punch scrunch
under	blunder plunder	thunder under	blood and thunder	loot and plunder
onder	wonder	boy wonder	no wonder	nine-day wonder
ung	bung clung dung flung	hung rung slung sprung	strung stung sung swung	wrung far-flung unsung highly-strung
ongue	tongue forked tongue sharp tongue hold your tongue	lost your tongue mother tongue slip of the tongue	tip of the tongue	
oung	young			

unk				
	bunk	flunk	skunk	tree trunk
	chunk	funk	slunk	
	clunk	junk	sunk	
	drunk	punk	trunk	
	dunk	shrunk	chipmunk	
onk	monk			
unt	blunt	punt	stunt	manhunt
	grunt	runt	bear hunt	witch hunt
	hunt	shunt	fox hunt	treasure hunt
ont	front	in front	seafront	back to front
up	cup	dress up	make-up	toss-up
	pup	fed up	mix-up	wind up
	up	fry-up	pick-up	buttercup
	back up	grown-up	press-up	coffee cup
	break-up	hard-up	round up	cover-up
	built-up	hiccup	slip-up	giddy-up
	checkup	ketchup	teacup	runner-up
	close-up	lock-up	throw up	washing up

My teacher has a sharp tongue –
She can cut through any nonsense!

Mum told me to hold my tongue –
But it was far too slippery!

'Have you lost your tongue?' asked the teacher.
I checked – it was still there, nestling in my mouth.

I made a slip of the tongue –
But managed not to fall over.

U -ur to -urn

ur	blur cur	fur slur	spur concur	demur occur
er	her	per	prefer	transfer
ere	were			
ir	fir	sir	stir	astir
urk	lurk	Turk		
erk	jerk	perk	berserk	go berserk
irk	irk	quirk	shirk	smirk
ork	work artwork clockwork firework	framework guesswork homework network	teamwork waxwork woodwork dirty work	donkey work handiwork hard at work overwork
url	curl	hurl	uncurl	unfurl
earl	earl	pearl	mother-of-pearl	
irl	girl	swirl	twirl	whirl
urn	burn spurn	turn urn	good turn return	sunburn U-turn
earn	earn	learn	yearn	live and learn
ern	fern	stern	concern	

-urred to -urse

I overheard –
the cat that purred,
for it preferred
the blackest bird.
Sadly now,
the rarest bird.

urred	blurred	purred	slurred	spurred
eard	heard	unheard	overheard	have you heard?
erd	herd	nerd	cowherd	goatherd
ird	bird third blackbird bluebird	firebird jailbird lovebird one-third	rare bird songbird early bird hummingbird	ladybird mockingbird whirlybird free as a bird
ord	word buzzword crossword	last word password swearword	break your word mum's the word	not a word word for word
urd	curd	absurd	lemon curd	
urse	curse	nurse	purse	reimburse
erse	verse adverse	converse disperse	diverse immerse	reverse universe
orse	worse	worse and worse		

U -urt to -use

urt
blurt curt hurt spurt

ert
pert alert desert expert
advert concert dessert

irt
dirt shirt squirt T-shirt
flirt skirt sweatshirt miniskirt

us
bus cactus walrus platypus
plus crocus genius thesaurus
pus minus radius apparatus
thus rumpus minibus Diplodocus
us schoolbus octopus hocus-pocus
bonus virus papyrus hippopotamus

ous
anxious raucous furious ravenous
callous wondrous glorious serious
famous courageous hideous stupendous
gorgeous curious horrendous tremendous
jealous dubious ludicrous various
monstrous enormous mischievous hilarious
nervous envious numerous ingenious
precious fabulous obvious mysterious

uss
fuss suss discuss kick up a fuss

use
fuse use confuse excuse
muse accuse defuse peruse
ruse amuse enthuse refuse

ews
news stews cashews interviews

oos
boos zoos tattoos kangaroos

ose
choose lose whose win or lose

ush	blush	hush	shush	hairbrush
	brush	lush	slush	hush-hush
	crush	mush	thrush	paintbrush
	flush	plush	bulrush	songthrush
	gush	rush	gold rush	toothbrush
usk	busk	husk	rusk	corn husk
	dusk	musk	tusk	dawn to dusk
ust	bust	must	disgust	stardust
	crust	rust	go bust	unjust
	dust	thrust	gold dust	bite the dust
	gust	trust	mistrust	dry as dust
	just	adjust	sawdust	like gold dust
ussed	bussed	fussed	discussed	nonplussed
ut	but	rut	doughnut	walnut
	cut	scut	haircut	coconut
	glut	shut	half-shut	halibut
	gut	smut	peanut	hazelnut
	hut	strut	rebut	in a rut
	jut	beechnut	shortcut	undercut
	nut	chestnut	tough nut	uppercut
	phut	clear-cut	tut-tut	open and shut
utt	butt	mutt	putt	ugly mutt

Danny's dog
was an ugly mutt –
Too much hair
in need of a cut.
Shaved him bald
Like a coconut ...
Tut. Tut. Tut!

U -ute to -uzzle

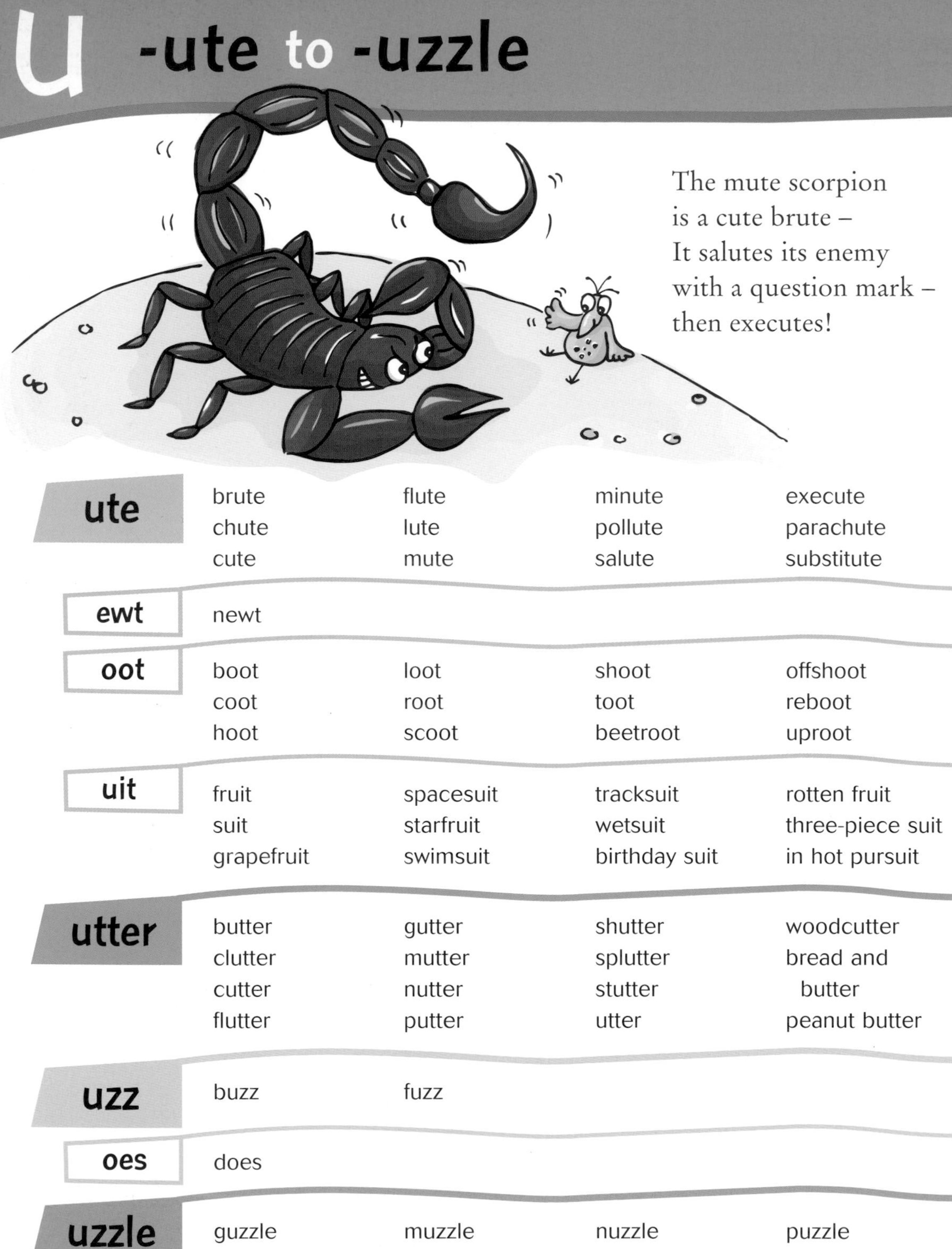

The mute scorpion
is a cute brute –
It salutes its enemy
with a question mark –
then executes!

ute	brute chute cute	flute lute mute	minute pollute salute	execute parachute substitute
ewt	newt			
oot	boot coot hoot	loot root scoot	shoot toot beetroot	offshoot reboot uproot
uit	fruit suit grapefruit	spacesuit starfruit swimsuit	tracksuit wetsuit birthday suit	rotten fruit three-piece suit in hot pursuit
utter	butter clutter cutter flutter	gutter mutter nutter putter	shutter splutter stutter utter	woodcutter bread and butter peanut butter
uzz	buzz	fuzz		
oes	does			
uzzle	guzzle	muzzle	nuzzle	puzzle

Index

a

aardvark / **-ark** 22
abbreviate / **-ate** 25
abcess / **-ess** 42
ablaze / **-aze** 28
able / **-able** 8
aboard / **-oard** 62
about / **-out** 83
abreast / **-est** 43
abroad / **-oard** 62
abstract / **-act** 11
absurd / **-urred** 95
abuse / **-oose** 74
accelerate / **-ate** 25
accept / **-ept** 42
access / **-ess** 42
acclaim / **-ame** 18
accomplice / **-iss** 58
account / **-ount** 82
accuse / **-use** 96
ace / **-ace** 9
ache / **-ake** 16
achieve / **-eve** 44
a-choo / **-oo** 70
acorn / **-orn** 78
acrobat / **-at** 24
acrobatic / **-ick** 46
across / **-oss** 80
act / **-act** 11
AD / **-e** 29
add / **-ad** 12
address / **-ess** 42
addressed / **-est** 43
adjoin / **-oin** 65
adjust / **-ust** 97
admit / **-it** 59
ado / **-oo** 70
adore / **-ore** 76
adored / **-oard** 62
adores / **-ores** 77
adorn / **-orn** 78
adrift / **-ift** 50
advance / **-ance** 19
adverse / **-urse** 95
advert / **-urt** 96
advertise / **-ies** 49
advice / **-ice** 46
advise / **-ies** 49
aerobics / **-icks** 47
aerodrome / **-ome** 68
aerofoil / **-oil** 65
aeroplane / **-ane** 20
afar / **-a** 8
afford / **-oard** 62
afloat / **-oat** 63
afraid / **-ade** 12
afresh / **-esh** 42
afternoon / **-oon** 73
afterthought / **-ort** 79
again / **-ane** 20
agape / **-ape** 21
age / **-age** 13
aggro / **-o** 61
aghast / **-ast** 24
agile / **-ile** 52
ago / **-o** 61
agog / **-og** 65
agree / **-e** 29
agreed / **-eed** 36
agrees / **-ees** 38
aground / **-ound** 82
aha / **-a** 8
ahead / **-ed** 35
ahoy / **-oy** 86
ail / **-ale** 14
aim / **-ame** 18
air / **-air** 15
airbed / **-ed** 35
airborne / **-orn** 78
aircraft / **-aft** 13
airline / **-ine** 55
airlock / **-ock** 64
airlocks / **-ocks** 64
airmail / **-ale** 14
airport / **-ort** 79
airspace / **-ace** 9
airspeed / **-eed** 36
airstrip / **-ip** 57
airtight / **-ight** 51
airy / **-airy** 16
aisle / **-ile** 52
ajar / **-a** 8
alarm / **-arm** 23
albatross / **-oss** 80
ale / **-ale** 14
alert / **-urt** 96
alibi / **-i** 45
alike / **-ike** 51
alive / **-ive** 60
all / **-all** 17
alley / **-alley** 17
alleyway / **-ay** 27
alleyways / **-aze** 28
alligator / **-ator** 26
allow / **-ow** 83
allowed / **-oud** 82
alloy / **-oy** 86
ally / **-i** 45
almost / **-ost** 80
alone / **-one** 69
along / **-ong** 69
alongside / **-ide** 48
aloud / **-oud** 82
alphabet / **-et** 44
alpine / **-ine** 55
although / **-o** 61
altitude / **-ude** 88
always / **-aze** 28
am / **-am** 17
amaze / **-aze** 28
amen / **-en** 40
amiss / **-iss** 58
ammo / **-o** 61
ammonite / **-ight** 51
amount / **-ount** 82
amuse / **-use** 96
amusing / **-ing** 56
anagram / **-am** 17
analogue / **-og** 65
and / **-and** 19
anecdote / **-oat** 63
angle / **-angle** 20
anklebone / **-one** 69
annoy / **-oy** 86
annoys / **-oise** 66
anon / **-on** 68
anorak / **-ack** 10
anoraks / **-acks** 11
ant / **-ant** 21
anteater / **-eater** 33
antelope / **-ope** 75
anthill / **-ill** 52
antic / **-antic** 21
antics / **-icks** 47
antidote / **-oat** 63
antifreeze / **-ees** 38
antique / **-eek** 37
antonym / **-im** 53
anvil / **-ill** 52
anxious / **-us** 96
anyhow / **-ow** 83
anyone / **-un** 92
anything / **-ing** 56
anytime / **-ime** 54
anyway / **-ay** 27
anywhere / **-air** 15
apart / **-art** 23
ape / **-ape** 21
apologise / **-ies** 49
apparatus / **-us** 96
appeal / **-eal** 30
appear / **-ear** 31
appendix / **-icks** 47
appetite / **-ight** 51
applause / **-ores** 77
appoint / **-oint** 65
appreciate / **-ate** 25
apprehend / **-end** 41
apprentice / **-iss** 58
apricot / **-ot** 81
arcade / **-ade** 12
arch / **-arch** 22
archway / **-ay** 27
are / **-a** 8
argue / **-oo** 71
argued / **-ude** 88
arise / **-ies** 49
aristocrat / **-at** 24
ark / **-ark** 22
arm / **-arm** 23
armadillo / **-o** 61
armband / **-and** 19
armchair / **-air** 15
armful / **-ul** 90
armhole / **-ole** 67
armpit / **-it** 59
around / **-ound** 82
arrayed / **-ade** 12
arrest / **-est** 43
arrive / **-ive** 60

arrow / **-o** 61
arrowhead / **-ed** 35
arrows / **-ows** 85
art / **-art** 23
artefact / **-act** 11
artwork / **-urk** 94
ascend / **-end** 41
ascent / **-ent** 41
ash / **-ash** 23
ashore / **-ore** 76
aside / **-ide** 48
ask / **-ask** 23
askew / **-oo** 70
asleep / **-eep** 38
assassinate / **-ate** 25
asterisk / **-isk** 58
astir / **-ur** 94
astound / **-ound** 82
astride / **-ide** 48
astronaut / **-ort** 79
asylum / **-um** 90
at / **-at** 24
ate / **-ate** 25
athlete / **-eat** 32
Atlantic / **-antic** 21
atmosphere / **-ear** 31
attach / **-atch** 24
attack / **-ack** 10
attacked / **-act** 11
attacks / **-acks** 11
attend / **-end** 41
attic / **-ick** 46
attitude / **-ude** 88
attract / **-act** 11
autograph / **-arf** 22
automatic / **-ick** 46
automobile / **-eal** 30
avenue / **-oo** 71
await / **-ate** 25
awake / **-ake** 16
award / **-oard** 62
aware / **-air** 15
away / **-ay** 27
awhile / **-ile** 52
awoke / **-oke** 66
axe / **-acks** 11
axis / **-iss** 58
aye aye / **-i** 45

baa / **-a** 8
babble / **-abble** 8
baboon / **-oon** 73
babyhood / **-ood** 72
babysat / **-at** 24
babysit / **-it** 59
babysitter / **-itter** 60
back / **-ack** 10
backache / **-ake** 16
backbend / **-end** 41
backbone / **-one** 69
backed / **-act** 11
backfire / **-ire** 57
background / **-ound** 82
backhand / **-and** 19
backlash / **-ash** 23
backlog / **-og** 65
backpack / **-ack** 10
backpacked / **-act** 11
backpacks / **-acks** 11
backs / **-acks** 11
backseat / **-eat** 32
backside / **-ide** 48
backstage / **-age** 13
backstreet / **-eat** 32
backtrack / **-ack** 10
backtracked / **-act** 11
backtracks / **-acks** 11
bad / **-ad** 12
bag / **-ag** 13
bagpipe / **-ipe** 57
baguette / **-et** 44
bail / **-ale** 14
bait / **-ate** 25
bake / **-ake** 16
balderdash / **-ash** 23
bale / **-ale** 14
ball / **-all** 17
ballboy / **-oy** 86
ballboys / **-oise** 66
ballet / **-ay** 27
ballgown / **-own** 84
balloon / **-oon** 73
ballroom / **-oom** 73
bamboo / **-oo** 70
ban / **-an** 18
band / **-and** 19
bandit / **-it** 59
bandstand / **-and** 19
bane / **-ane** 20

bang / **-ang** 20
bangle / **-angle** 20
banjo / **-o** 61
banjos / **-ows** 85
bank / **-ank** 21
banned / **-and** 19
bap / **-ap** 21
bar / **-a** 8
barbecue / **-oo** 71
barbecued / **-ude** 88
barcode / **-oad** 62
bare / **-air** 15
bareback / **-ack** 10
barefaced / **-aced** 9
barefoot / **-oot** 74
bargepole / **-ole** 67
bark / **-ark** 22
barred / **-ard** 22
barricade / **-ade** 12
base / **-ace** 9
baseball / **-all** 17
bash / **-ash** 23
basic / **-ick** 46
bask / **-ask** 23
basket / **-it** 59
basketball / **-all** 17
bassoon / **-oon** 73
bat / **-at** 24
bathroom / **-oom** 73
bathtub / **-ub** 87
baton / **-on** 68
batter / **-atter** 26
battle / **-attle** 26
battleship / **-ip** 57
batty / **-atty** 26
bawl / **-all** 17
bay / **-ay** 27
bays / **-aze** 28
bazaar / **-a** 8
BC / **-e** 29
be / **-e** 29
bead / **-eed** 36
beak / **-eek** 37
beam / **-eam** 30
bean / **-een** 37
beanbag / **-ag** 13
beanfeast / **-east** 32
beanpole / **-ole** 67
beanstalk / **-ork** 78
bear / **-air** 15
bearskin / **-in** 54
beast / **-east** 32
beat / **-eat** 32

beater / **-eater** 33
beautiful / **-ul** 90
became / **-ame** 18
beck / **-eck** 33
become / **-um** 90
bed / **-ed** 35
bedbug / **-ug** 89
bedpost / **-ost** 80
bedroom / **-oom** 73
bedside / **-ide** 48
bedspread / **-ed** 35
bedstead / **-ed** 35
bedtime / **-ime** 54
bee / **-e** 29
beechnut / **-ut** 97
beef / **-eaf** 30
beefsteak / **-ake** 16
beehive / **-ive** 60
beeline / **-ine** 55
been / **-een** 37
beep / **-eep** 38
beer / **-ear** 31
bees / **-ees** 38
beeswax / **-acks** 11
beetroot / **-ute** 98
before / **-ore** 76
beforehand / **-and** 19
befriend / **-end** 41
beg / **-eg** 39
began / **-an** 18
begin / **-in** 54
begrudge / **-udge** 89
begun / **-un** 92
behalf / **-arf** 22
behave / **-ave** 27
behead / **-ed** 35
behind / **-ind** 55
belief / **-eaf** 30
believe / **-eve** 44
bell / **-ell** 39
bellow / **-ello** 39
bellows / **-ows** 85
bellyache / **-ake** 16
bellyflop / **-op** 75
belong / **-ong** 69
below / **-o** 61
belt / **-elt** 40
bench / **-ench** 40
bend / **-end** 41
bent / **-ent** 41
bequest / **-est** 43
beret / **-ay** 27
berry / **-erry** 42

berserk / **-urk** 94
bespatter / **-atter** 26
best / **-est** 43
bet / **-et** 44
Bethlehem / **-em** 40
betray / **-ay** 27
betrayed / **-ade** 12
betrays / **-aze** 28
between / **-een** 37
beware / **-air** 15
bewitch / **-itch** 60
beyond / **-ond** 69
bib / **-ib** 46
bid / **-id** 47
biff / **-iff** 49
biffed / **-ift** 50
big / **-ig** 50
bigwig / **-ig** 50
bike / **-ike** 51
bill / **-ill** 52
billionaire / **-air** 15
bin / **-in** 54
bind / **-ind** 55
binge / **-inge** 56
bingo / **-o** 61
bionic / **-ick** 46
biosphere / **-ear** 31
bird / **-urred** 95
birdcage / **-age** 13
birdcall / **-all** 17
birdseed / **-eed** 36
birthday / **-ay** 27
birthdays / **-aze** 28
birthplace / **-ace** 9
biscuit / **-it** 59
bit / **-it** 59
bite / **-ight** 51
bitter / **-itter** 60
bittersweet / **-eat** 32
blab / **-ab** 8
black / **-ack** 10
blackberry / **-erry** 42
blackbird / **-urred** 95
blacked / **-act** 11
blackhead / **-ed** 35
blackmail / **-ale** 14
blackout / **-out** 83
blade / **-ade** 12
blame / **-ame** 18
blank / **-ank** 21
blare / **-air** 15
blast / **-ast** 24
blaze / **-aze** 28
bleak / **-eek** 37
bleat / **-eat** 32
bled / **-ed** 35
bleed / **-eed** 36
bleep / **-eep** 38
blend / **-end** 41
blender / **-ender** 41
bless / **-ess** 42
blessed / **-est** 43
blew / **-oo** 70
blind / **-ind** 55
blindfold / **-old** 66
blink / **-ink** 56
blip / **-ip** 57
bliss / **-iss** 58
blob / **-ob** 63
block / **-ock** 64
blocks / **-ocks** 64
bloke / **-oke** 66
blond / **-ond** 69
blood / **-ud** 88
bloodhound / **-ound** 82
bloodshed / **-ed** 35
bloodshot / **-ot** 81
bloodstream / **-eam** 30
bloom / **-oom** 73
blot / **-ot** 81
blow / **-o** 61
blown / **-one** 69
blows / **-ows** 85
blue / **-oo** 71
bluebell / **-ell** 39
blueberry / **-erry** 42
bluebird / **-urred** 95
blueprint / **-int** 57
bluetit / **-it** 59
bluff / **-uff** 89
blunder / **-under** 92
blunt / **-unt** 93
blur / **-ur** 94
blurred / **-urred** 95
blurt / **-urt** 96
blush / **-ush** 97
boar / **-ore** 76
board / **-oard** 62
boars / **-ores** 77
boast / **-ost** 80
boastful / **-ul** 90
boat / **-oat** 63
boatload / **-oad** 62
bob / **-ob** 63
bobble / **-obble** 63
bobsled / **-ed** 35
bobsleigh / **-ay** 27
bodyguard / **-ard** 22
bog / **-og** 65
boil / **-oil** 65
bold / **-old** 66
bolt / **-olt** 67
bombard / **-ard** 22
bombshell / **-ell** 39
bond / **-ond** 69
bone / **-one** 69
bonfire / **-ire** 57
bong / **-ong** 69
bongo / **-o** 61
bongos / **-ows** 85
bonus / **-us** 96
boo / **-oo** 70
booed / **-ude** 88
boo-hoo / **-oo** 70
boo-hooed / **-ude** 88
book / **-ook** 72
bookcase / **-ace** 9
bookmark / **-ark** 22
bookshop / **-op** 75
bookstall / **-all** 17
boom / **-oom** 73
boomerang / **-ang** 20
boos / **-use** 96
boot / **-ute** 98
bop / **-op** 75
borderline / **-ine** 55
bore / **-ore** 76
bored / **-oard** 62
bores / **-ores** 77
boring / **-ing** 56
born / **-orn** 78
borne / **-orn** 78
boss / **-oss** 80
bottleneck / **-eck** 33
bottlenecks / **-ecks** 34
bough / **-ow** 83
bought / **-ort** 79
bound / **-ound** 82
bouquet / **-ay** 27
bout / **-out** 83
boutique / **-eek** 37
bow / **-o** 61
bow / **-ow** 83
bowed / **-oud** 82
bowel / **-owl** 84
bowl / **-ole** 67
bows / **-ows** 85
bow-wow / **-ow** 83
bow-wowed / **-oud** 82
box / **-ocks** 64
boy / **-oy** 86
boyfriend / **-end** 41
boyhood / **-ood** 72
boys / **-oise** 66
brace / **-ace** 9
braced / **-aced** 9
bracelet / **-it** 59
brag / **-ag** 13
braid / **-ade** 12
brain / **-ane** 20
brainstorm / **-orm** 78
brainwash / **-osh** 80
brainwave / **-ave** 27
brake / **-ake** 16
bran / **-an** 18
brand / **-and** 19
brandish / **-ish** 58
brash / **-ash** 23
brass / **-ass** 24
brat / **-at** 24
brave / **-ave** 27
bravo / **-o** 61
brawl / **-all** 17
bray / **-ay** 27
brayed / **-ade** 12
brays / **-aze** 28
bread / **-ed** 35
break / **-ake** 16
breakdown / **-own** 84
breakneck / **-eck** 33
breakout / **-out** 83
breakthrough / **-oo** 70
breast / **-est** 43
breaststroke / **-oke** 66
bred / **-ed** 35
breed / **-eed** 36
breeze / **-ees** 38
breezy / **-easy** 32
brew / **-oo** 70
brewed / **-ude** 88
bric-a-brac / **-ack** 10
brick / **-ick** 46
bricks / **-icks** 47
bride / **-ide** 48
bridegroom / **-oom** 73
bridesmaid / **-ade** 12
bridge / **-idge** 49
brief / **-eaf** 30
bright / **-ight** 51
brill / **-ill** 52
brim / **-im** 53
brine / **-ine** 55

bring / **-ing** 56
brink / **-ink** 56
brisk / **-isk** 58
broad / **-oard** 62
broil / **-oil** 65
broke / **-oke** 66
broncos / **-ows** 85
brook / **-ook** 72
broom / **-oom** 73
broomstick / **-ick** 46
broomsticks / **-icks** 47
brotherhood / **-ood** 72
brought / **-ort** 79
brow / **-ow** 83
brown / **-own** 84
browned / **-ound** 82
brunch / **-unch** 92
brunette / **-et** 44
brush / **-ush** 97
brute / **-ute** 98
bubble / **-ubble** 87
buccaneer / **-ear** 31
buck / **-uck** 87
bucket / **-it** 59
buckle / **-uckle** 88
bud / **-ud** 88
budge / **-udge** 89
buff / **-uff** 89
buffalo / **-o** 61
buffaloes / **-ows** 85
buffet / **-ay** 27
buffoon / **-oon** 73
bug / **-ug** 89
building / **-ing** 56
built / **-ilt** 53
bull / **-ul** 90
bulldog / **-og** 65
bulldoze / **-ows** 85
bullfight / **-ight** 51
bullfrog / **-og** 65
bullring / **-ing** 56
bulrush / **-ush** 97
bumblebee / **-e** 29
bumblebees / **-ees** 38
bump / **-ump** 91
bun / **-un** 92
bunch / **-unch** 92
bung / **-ung** 92
bungalow / **-o** 61
bungalows / **-ows** 85
bunk / **-unk** 93
buoy / **-oy** 86
buoys / **-oise** 66
burn / **-urn** 94
burrow / **-o** 61
burrowed / **-oad** 62
burrows / **-ows** 85
bury / **-erry** 42
bus / **-us** 96
busk / **-usk** 97
bussed / **-ust** 97
bust / **-ust** 97
but / **-ut** 97
butt / **-ut** 97
butter / **-utter** 98
buttercup / **-up** 93
butterflies / **-ies** 49
butterfly / **-i** 45
buttonhole / **-ole** 67
buy / **-i** 45
buzz / **-uzz** 98
buzzword / **-urred** 95
by / **-i** 45
bye / **-i** 45
bypass / **-ass** 24
byte / **-ight** 51

C

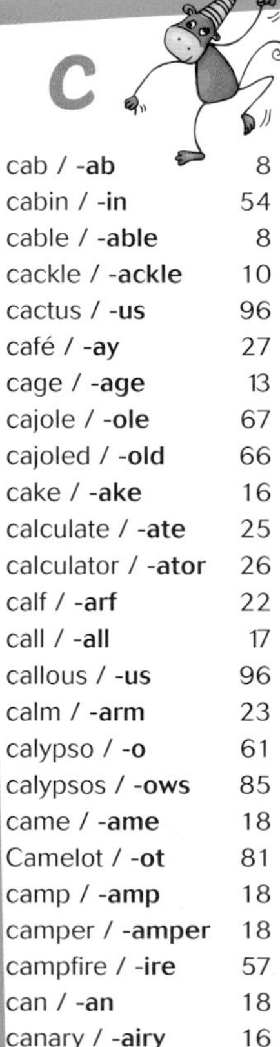

cab / **-ab** 8
cabin / **-in** 54
cable / **-able** 8
cackle / **-ackle** 10
cactus / **-us** 96
café / **-ay** 27
cage / **-age** 13
cajole / **-ole** 67
cajoled / **-old** 66
cake / **-ake** 16
calculate / **-ate** 25
calculator / **-ator** 26
calf / **-arf** 22
call / **-all** 17
callous / **-us** 96
calm / **-arm** 23
calypso / **-o** 61
calypsos / **-ows** 85
came / **-ame** 18
Camelot / **-ot** 81
camp / **-amp** 18
camper / **-amper** 18
campfire / **-ire** 57
can / **-an** 18
canary / **-airy** 16
candlelight / **-ight** 51
candlestick / **-ick** 46
candlesticks / **-icks** 47
candyfloss / **-oss** 80
cane / **-ane** 20
canine / **-ine** 55
canned / **-and** 19
cannonball / **-all** 17
cannot / **-ot** 81
canoe / **-oo** 70
canteen / **-een** 37
cap / **-ap** 21
cape / **-ape** 21
Capricorn / **-orn** 78
capsize / **-ies** 49
capsule / **-ool** 72
car / **-a** 8
caramel / **-ell** 39
caravan / **-an** 18
card / **-ard** 22
cardboard / **-oard** 62
care / **-air** 15
career / **-ear** 31
carefree / **-e** 29
careful / **-ul** 90
caress / **-ess** 42
caressed / **-est** 43
caribou / **-oo** 70
carload / **-oad** 62
carnivore / **-ore** 76
carnivores / **-ores** 77
carousel / **-ell** 39
carpet / **-it** 59
cart / **-art** 23
carthorse / **-orse** 79
cartload / **-oad** 62
cartoon / **-oon** 73
cartwheel / **-eal** 30
carwash / **-osh** 80
case / **-ace** 9
cash / **-ash** 23
cashews / **-use** 96
cashier / **-ear** 31
cask / **-ask** 23
casserole / **-ole** 67
cassette / **-et** 44
cast / **-ast** 24
castaway / **-ay** 27
castaways / **-aze** 28
cat / **-at** 24
catalogue / **-og** 65
catamaran / **-an** 18
catch / **-atch** 24
cater / **-ator** 26
caterwaul / **-all** 17
catflap / **-ap** 21
catkin / **-in** 54
cattle / **-attle** 26
catty / **-atty** 26
catwalk / **-ork** 78
caught / **-ort** 79
cauliflower / **-ower** 84
cause / **-ores** 77
cavalcade / **-ade** 12
cavalier / **-ear** 31
cave / **-ave** 27
caveman / **-an** 18
caviar / **-a** 8
caw / **-ore** 76
CD / **-e** 29
cease / **-eece** 36
ceased / **-east** 32
ceiling / **-ing** 56
celebrate / **-ate** 25
cell / **-ell** 39
cellist / **-ist** 58
cello / **-ello** 39
Celt / **-elt** 40
cement / **-ent** 41
cent / **-ent** 41
centaur / **-ore** 76
centaurs / **-ores** 77
centigrade / **-ade** 12
centilitre / **-eater** 33
centimetre / **-eater** 33
centipede / **-eed** 36
CFC / **-e** 29
chain / **-ane** 20
chainmail / **-ale** 14
chainsaw / **-ore** 76
chair / **-air** 15
chalet / **-ay** 27
chalk / **-ork** 78
champ / **-amp** 18
championship / **-ip** 57
chance / **-ance** 19
chandelier / **-ear** 31
changeling / **-ing** 56
chants / **-ance** 19
chap / **-ap** 21
charcoal / **-ole** 67
charm / **-arm** 23
charred / **-ard** 22
chase / **-ace** 9
chat / **-at** 24
chatter / **-atter** 26

chatterbox / **-ocks** 64
chatty / **-atty** 26
cheap / **-eep** 25
cheapskate / **-ate** 25
cheat / **-eat** 32
check / **-eck** 33
checked / **-ect** 34
checklist / **-ist** 58
checkmate / **-ate** 25
checkpoint / **-oint** 65
checks / **-ecks** 34
checkup / **-up** 93
cheek / **-eek** 37
cheekbone / **-one** 69
cheep / **-eep** 38
cheer / **-ear** 31
cheerful / **-ul** 90
cheese / **-ees** 38
cheesecake / **-ake** 16
cheetah / **-eater** 33
cheque / **-eck** 33
cherry / **-erry** 42
cherub / **-ub** 87
chess / **-ess** 42
chessboard / **-oard** 62
chest / **-est** 43
chestnut / **-ut** 97
chew / **-oo** 70
chewed / **-ude** 88
chick / **-ick** 46
chickpea / **-e** 29
chickpeas / **-ees** 38
chicks / **-icks** 47
chief / **-eaf** 30
chihuahua / **-a** 8
child / **-ild** 52
childhood / **-ood** 72
childlike / **-ike** 51
chill / **-ill** 52
chilli / **-illy** 53
chilly / **-illy** 53
chime / **-ime** 54
chimney / **-e** 29
chimneys / **-ees** 38
chimneypot / **-ot** 81
chimpanzee / **-e** 29
chimpanzees / **-ees** 38
chin / **-in** 54
Chinese / **-ees** 38
chink / **-ink** 56
chinwag / **-ag** 13
chip / **-ip** 57
chipmunk / **-unk** 93
chitchat / **-at** 24
chlorine / **-een** 37
choirboy / **-oy** 86
choke / **-oke** 66
choose / **-use** 96
chop / **-op** 75
chopstick / **-ick** 46
chopsticks / **-icks** 47
chord / **-oard** 62
chore / **-ore** 76
chores / **-ores** 77
chose / **-ows** 85
chow mein / **-ane** 20
chrome / **-ome** 68
chrysalis / **-iss** 58
chuck / **-uck** 87
chuckle / **-uckle** 88
chug / **-ug** 89
chum / **-um** 90
chunk / **-unk** 93
chute / **-ute** 98
circuit / **-it** 59
citadel / **-ell** 39
citizen / **-en** 40
citizenship / **-ip** 57
clackity-clack / **-ack** 10
clad / **-ad** 12
claim / **-ame** 18
clam / **-am** 17
clamp / **-amp** 18
clan / **-an** 18
clang / **-ang** 20
clank / **-ank** 21
clap / **-ap** 21
clarinet / **-et** 44
clash / **-ash** 23
clasp / **-asp** 23
class / **-ass** 24
classed / **-ast** 24
classroom / **-oom** 73
clatter / **-atter** 26
claw / **-ore** 76
claws / **-ores** 77
clay / **-ay** 27
clean / **-een** 37
clear / **-ear** 31
clementine / **-een** 37
clench / **-ench** 40
click / **-ick** 46
clicks / **-icks** 47
cliff / **-iff** 49
climax / **-acks** 11
climb / **-ime** 54
clinch / **-inch** 55
cling / **-ing** 56
clink / **-ink** 56
clip / **-ip** 57
clipboard / **-oard** 62
clip-clop / **-op** 75
clique / **-eek** 37
cloak / **-oke** 66
cloakroom / **-oom** 73
clock / **-ock** 64
clocks / **-ocks** 64
clockwise / **-ies** 49
clockwork / **-urk** 94
clod / **-od** 65
clog / **-og** 65
clone / **-one** 69
close / **-ose** 80
close / **-ows** 85
clot / **-ot** 81
clothesline / **-ine** 55
clothing / **-ing** 56
cloud / **-oud** 82
clout / **-out** 83
cloverleaf / **-eaf** 30
clown / **-own** 84
clowned / **-ound** 82
club / **-ub** 87
cluck / **-uck** 87
clue / **-oo** 71
clump / **-ump** 91
clung / **-ung** 92
clunk / **-unk** 93
clutch / **-uch** 87
clutter / **-utter** 98
coarse / **-orse** 79
coast / **-ost** 80
coastguard / **-ard** 22
coastline / **-ine** 55
coat / **-oat** 63
cobblestone / **-one** 69
cock / **-ock** 64
cockatoo / **-oo** 70
cockleshell / **-ell** 39
cockpit / **-it** 59
cocky / **-ocky** 64
coconut / **-ut** 97
cocoon / **-oon** 73
cod / **-od** 65
code / **-oad** 62
coffee / **-e** 29
coffeepot / **-ot** 81
coffin / **-in** 54
cog / **-og** 65
coil / **-oil** 65
coin / **-oin** 65
cold / **-old** 66
coleslaw / **-ore** 76
collarbone / **-one** 69
collect / **-ect** 34
colourblind / **-ind** 55
colourful / **-ul** 90
colt / **-olt** 67
comb / **-ome** 68
combat / **-at** 24
combine / **-ine** 55
come / **-um** 90
comedown / **-own** 84
comic / **-ick** 46
comics / **-icks** 47
commando / **-o** 61
commonplace / **-ace** 9
commotion / **-otion** 81
communicate / **-ate** 25
compact / **-act** 11
compare / **-air** 15
compete / **-eat** 32
complain / **-ane** 20
complete / **-eat** 32
complicate / **-ate** 25
compliment / **-ent** 41
con / **-on** 68
conceal / **-eal** 30
concentrate / **-ate** 25
concern / **-urn** 94
concert / **-urt** 96
concise / **-ice** 46
Concorde / **-oard** 62
concourse / **-orse** 79
concur / **-ur** 94
condor / **-ore** 76
cone / **-one** 69
confess / **-ess** 42
confessed / **-est** 43
confiscate / **-ate** 25
confuse / **-use** 96
conman / **-an** 18
connect / **-ect** 34
conned / **-ond** 69
conquest / **-est** 43
consent / **-ent** 41
console / **-ole** 67
consoled / **-old** 66
contain / **-ane** 20
content / **-ent** 41
contest / **-est** 43
continue / **-oo** 71

contraband / **-and** 19
contract / **-act** 11
contrary / **-airy** 16
contrast / **-ast** 24
control / **-ole** 67
controlled / **-old** 66
converse / **-urse** 95
convoy / **-oy** 86
coo / **-oo** 70
cooed / **-ude** 88
cook / **-ook** 72
cookbook / **-ook** 72
cool / **-ool** 72
coop / **-oop** 74
cooperate / **-ate** 25
coot / **-ute** 98
cop / **-op** 75
cope / **-ope** 75
copycat / **-at** 24
copyright / **-ight** 51
cord / **-oard** 62
corduroy / **-oy** 86
core / **-ore** 76
cores / **-ores** 77
cork / **-ork** 78
corkscrew / **-oo** 70
corn / **-orn** 78
cornflower / **-ower** 84
correct / **-ect** 34
corridor / **-ore** 76
corridors / **-ores** 77
costume / **-oom** 73
cot / **-ot** 81
couch / **-ouch** 81
could / **-ood** 72
count / **-ount** 82
countdown / **-own** 84
counterfoil / **-oil** 65
countryside / **-ide** 48
coupon / **-on** 68
courageous / **-us** 96
courgette / **-et** 44
course / **-orse** 79
court / **-ort** 79
cow / **-ow** 83
cowardice / **-iss** 58
cowbell / **-ell** 39
cowboy / **-oy** 86
cowboys / **-oise** 66
cowed / **-oud** 82
cower / **-ower** 84
cowherd / **-urred** 95
cowpat / **-at** 24

cowslip / **-ip** 57
cox / **-ocks** 64
coy / **-oy** 86
crab / **-ab** 8
crabby / **-abby** 8
crack / **-ack** 10
crackdown / **-own** 84
cracked / **-act** 11
crackle / **-ackle** 10
crackpot / **-ot** 81
cracks / **-acks** 11
craft / **-aft** 13
crag / **-ag** 13
cram / **-am** 17
cramfull / **-ul** 90
cramp / **-amp** 18
crane / **-ane** 20
crank / **-ank** 21
crankshaft / **-aft** 13
crash / **-ash** 23
crash-land / **-and** 19
crate / **-ate** 25
crater / **-ator** 26
crave / **-ave** 27
crawl / **-all** 17
craze / **-aze** 28
creak / **-eek** 37
cream / **-eam** 30
crease / **-eece** 36
creased / **-east** 32
create / **-ate** 25
creator / **-ator** 26
creed / **-eed** 36
creek / **-eek** 37
creep / **-eep** 38
crept / **-ept** 42
cress / **-ess** 42
crest / **-est** 43
crew / **-oo** 70
crib / **-ib** 46
cricket / **-it** 59
cried / **-ide** 48
cries / **-ies** 49
crime / **-ime** 54
cringe / **-inge** 56
crispbread / **-ed** 35
croak / **-oke** 66
crock / **-ock** 64
crocodile / **-ile** 52
crocus / **-us** 96
crone / **-one** 69
crook / **-ook** 72
croon / **-oon** 73

crop / **-op** 75
croquette / **-et** 44
cross / **-oss** 80
crossbar / **-a** 8
crossbow / **-o** 61
crossbows / **-ows** 85
crosspatch / **-atch** 24
crossword / **-urred** 95
crouch / **-ouch** 81
crow / **-o** 61
crowbar / **-a** 8
crowd / **-oud** 82
crowed / **-oad** 62
crown / **-own** 84
crowned / **-ound** 82
crows / **-ows** 85
crude / **-ude** 88
crumb / **-um** 90
crumble / **-umble** 91
crummy / **-ummy** 91
crunch / **-unch** 92
crush / **-ush** 97
crust / **-ust** 97
crutch / **-uch** 87
cry / **-i** 45
cub / **-ub** 87
cubbyhole / **-ole** 67
cuckoo / **-oo** 70
cuddle / **-uddle** 88
cue / **-oo** 71
cued / **-ude** 88
cuff / **-uff** 89
cuisine / **-een** 37
cul-de-sac / **-ack** 10
culprit / **-it** 59
cunning / **-ing** 56
cup / **-up** 93
cupful / **-ul** 90
cur / **-ur** 94
curd / **-urred** 95
curious / **-us** 96
curl / **-url** 94
currycomb / **-ome** 68
curse / **-urse** 95
curt / **-urt** 96
cut / **-ut** 97
cute / **-ute** 98
cut-rate / **-ate** 25
cutter / **-utter** 98
cyclist / **-ist** 58
Czech / **-eck** 33

d

dab / **-ab** 8
dabble / **-abble** 8
dad / **-ad** 12
daffodil / **-ill** 52
daft / **-aft** 13
dairy / **-airy** 16
dale / **-ale** 14
dam / **-am** 17
damp / **-amp** 18
damper / **-amper** 18
dance / **-ance** 19
dandruff / **-uff** 89
dangle / **-angle** 20
dank / **-ank** 21
dare / **-air** 15
dark / **-ark** 22
dart / **-art** 23
dartboard / **-oard** 62
dash / **-ash** 23
dashboard / **-oard** 62
database / **-ace** 9
date / **-ate** 25
dawn / **-orn** 78
day / **-ay** 27
daybreak / **-ake** 16
daydream / **-eam** 30
day-dreaming / **-ing** 56
daylight / **-ight** 51
days / **-aze** 28
daytime / **-ime** 54
daze / **-aze** 28
DC / **-e** 29
dead / **-ed** 35
deadbeat / **-eat** 32
deadlock / **-ock** 64
deadpan / **-an** 18
deal / **-eal** 30
dear / **-ear** 31
deathbed / **-ed** 35
debate / **-ate** 25
decade / **-ade** 12
decay / **-ay** 27
decayed / **-ade** 12
deceased / **-east** 32
deceive / **-eve** 44
decide / **-ide** 48
deck / **-eck** 33
decks / **-ecks** 34
declare / **-air** 15

decompose / **-ows** 85
decorate / **-ate** 25
decoy / **-oy** 86
decrease / **-eece** 36
decreased / **-east** 32
decrees / **-ees** 38
deduce / **-oose** 74
deed / **-eed** 36
deep / **-eep** 38
deer / **-ear** 31
deface / **-ace** 9
defaced / **-aced** 9
defeat / **-eat** 32
defence / **-ence** 40
defend / **-end** 41
defender / **-ender** 41
defuse / **-use** 96
degree / **-e** 29
degrees / **-ees** 38
delay / **-ay** 27
delayed / **-ade** 12
delays / **-aze** 28
delete / **-eat** 32
deliberate / **-ate** 25
delight / **-ight** 51
deliver / **-iver** 60
deliveryman / **-an** 18
demonstrate / **-ate** 25
demur / **-ur** 94
den / **-en** 40
denied / **-ide** 48
denim / **-im** 53
dense / **-ence** 40
dent / **-ent** 41
deny / **-i** 45
depart / **-art** 23
depend / **-end** 41
depress / **-ess** 42
depressed / **-est** 43
descend / **-end** 41
descent / **-ent** 41
desert / **-urt** 96
design / **-ine** 55
desire / **-ire** 57
despair / **-air** 15
dessert / **-urt** 96
destroy / **-oy** 86
destroys / **-oise** 66
detach / **-atch** 24
detail / **-ale** 14
detect / **-ect** 34
detest / **-est** 43
detonate / **-ate** 25
deuce / **-oose** 74
devote / **-oat** 63
devotion / **-otion** 81
devour / **-ower** 84
dew / **-oo** 70
dhow / **-ow** 83
diagram / **-am** 17
dial / **-ile** 52
dialect / **-ect** 34
dialogue / **-og** 65
dice / **-ice** 46
dictator / **-ator** 26
did / **-id** 47
diddle / **-iddle** 47
didgeridoo / **-oo** 70
die / **-i** 45
died / **-ide** 48
dies / **-ies** 49
dig / **-ig** 50
digest / **-est** 43
digress / **-ess** 42
digressed / **-est** 43
dill / **-ill** 52
dilly-dally / **-alley** 17
dim / **-im** 53
dime / **-ime** 54
dine / **-ine** 55
dined / **-ind** 55
dingbat / **-at** 24
ding-dong / **-ong** 69
dinnertime / **-ime** 54
dinosaur / **-ore** 76
dinosaurs / **-ores** 77
dip / **-ip** 57
Diplodocus / **-us** 96
dire / **-ipe** 57
direct / **-ect** 34
dirt / **-urt** 96
disagree / **-e** 29
disagreed / **-eed** 36
disagrees / **-ees** 38
disappear / **-ear** 31
disappoint / **-oint** 65
disarm / **-arm** 23
disbelieve / **-eve** 44
disco / **-o** 61
disconnect / **-ect** 34
discontent / **-ent** 41
discotheque / **-eck** 33
discount / **-ount** 82
discreet / **-eat** 32
discuss / **-us** 96
discussed / **-ust** 97
disease / **-ees** 38
disgrace / **-ace** 9
disgraced / **-aced** 9
disguise / **-ies** 49
disgust / **-ust** 97
dish / **-ish** 58
disk / **-isk** 58
dislike / **-ike** 51
disloyal / **-oil** 65
dismiss / **-iss** 58
dismissed / **-ist** 58
disobey / **-ay** 27
disobeyed / **-ade** 12
disperse / **-urse** 95
displaced / **-aced** 9
displayed / **-ade** 12
disrespect / **-ect** 34
distract / **-act** 11
distraught / **-ort** 79
distress / **-ess** 42
distressed / **-est** 43
ditch / **-itch** 60
ditto / **-o** 61
dive / **-ive** 60
diverse / **-urse** 95
divide / **-ide** 48
divine / **-ine** 55
divorce / **-orse** 79
do / **-oo** 70
dock / **-ock** 64
docks / **-ocks** 64
dodo / **-o** 61
doe / **-o** 61
does / **-uzz** 98
dog / **-og** 65
doghouse / **-ouse** 83
doing / **-ing** 56
dole / **-ole** 67
dolphin / **-in** 54
dome / **-ome** 68
dominoes / **-ows** 85
don / **-on** 68
done / **-un** 92
dong / **-ong** 69
donkey / **-e** 29
donkeys / **-ees** 38
donned / **-ond** 69
doom / **-oom** 73
door jamb / **-am** 17
door / **-ore** 76
doorbell / **-ell** 39
doorknob / **-ob** 63
doormat / **-at** 24
doors / **-ores** 77
doorway / **-ay** 27
doorways / **-aze** 28
dormouse / **-ouse** 83
dose / **-ose** 80
dot / **-ot** 81
dote / **-oat** 63
dotty / **-otty** 81
double / **-ubble** 87
doublecross / **-oss** 80
doubt / **-out** 83
doubtful / **-ul** 90
dough / **-o** 61
doughnut / **-ut** 97
douse / **-ouse** 83
dovecot / **-ot** 81
down / **-own** 84
downcast / **-ast** 24
downed / **-ound** 82
downfall / **-all** 17
downhill / **-ill** 52
downpour / **-ore** 76
downriver / **-iver** 60
downstream / **-eam** 30
doze / **-ows** 85
drab / **-ab** 8
drag / **-ag** 13
dragnet / **-et** 44
dragonflies / **-ies** 49
dragonfly / **-i** 45
drain / **-ane** 20
drainpipe / **-ipe** 57
drake / **-ake** 16
drank / **-ank** 21
drape / **-ape** 21
draught / **-aft** 13
draw / **-ore** 76
drawback / **-ack** 10
drawbridge / **-idge** 49
drawers / **-ores** 77
drawl / **-all** 17
drawn / **-orn** 78
draws / **-ores** 77
dread / **-ed** 35
dreadful / **-ul** 90
dreadlocks / **-ocks** 64
dreadnought / **-ort** 79
dream / **-eam** 30
dreamland / **-and** 19
dredge / **-edge** 35
dreg / **-eg** 39
drench / **-ench** 40
dress / **-ess** 42

dressed / **-est** 43
drew / **-oo** 70
dribble / **-ibble** 46
dried / **-ide** 48
dries / **-ies** 49
drift / **-ift** 50
driftwood / **-ood** 72
drill / **-ill** 52
drink / **-ink** 56
drip / **-ip** 57
drive / **-ive** 60
drone / **-one** 69
drool / **-ool** 72
droop / **-oop** 74
drop / **-op** 75
dropout / **-out** 83
drought / **-out** 83
drown / **-own** 84
drowned / **-ound** 82
drudge / **-udge** 89
drug / **-ug** 89
drum / **-um** 90
drumbeat / **-eat** 32
drumstick / **-ick** 46
drumsticks / **-icks** 47
drunk / **-unk** 93
dry / **-i** 45
dubious / **-us** 96
duck / **-uck** 87
duckling / **-ing** 56
duckweed / **-eed** 36
dud / **-ud** 88
due / **-oo** 71
duet / **-et** 44
duff / **-uff** 89
dug / **-ug** 89
dumb / **-um** 90
dumbbell / **-ell** 39
dumbfound / **-ound** 82
dumbstruck / **-uck** 87
dummy / **-ummy** 91
dump / **-ump** 91
dune / **-oon** 73
dung / **-ung** 92
dungarees / **-ees** 38
dunk / **-unk** 93
dupe / **-oop** 74
duplicate / **-ate** 25
duress / **-ess** 42
dusk / **-usk** 97
dust / **-ust** 97
dustbin / **-in** 54
dustcart / **-art** 23
dustpan / **-an** 18
Dutch / **-uch** 87
duvet / **-ay** 27
DVD / **-e** 29
dwell / **-ell** 39
dwelt / **-elt** 40
dye / **-i** 45
dynamite / **-ight** 51
dynamos / **-ows** 85

ear / **-ear** 31
earache / **-ake** 16
eardrum / **-um** 90
earl / **-url** 94
earlobe / **-obe** 64
earmark / **-ark** 22
earmuff / **-uff** 89
earn / **-urn** 94
earplug / **-ug** 89
earring / **-ing** 56
earshot / **-ot** 81
earthbound / **-ound** 82
earthquake / **-ake** 16
earwax / **-acks** 11
earwig / **-ig** 50
ease / **-ees** 38
east / **-east** 32
eastbound / **-ound** 82
easy / **-easy** 32
easy-peasy / **-easy** 32
eat / **-eat** 32
eater / **-eater** 33
eavesdrop / **-op** 75
echo / **-o** 61
éclair / **-air** 15
edge / **-edge** 35
educate / **-ate** 25
eek! / **-eek** 37
eel / **-eal** 30
effect / **-ect** 34
egg / **-eg** 39
eggbeater / **-eater** 33
egghead / **-ed** 35
eggshell / **-ell** 39
eiderdown / **-own** 84
eight / **-ate** 25
eighteen / **-een** 37
eject / **-ect** 34
elastic / **-ick** 46
elbow / **-o** 61
elbowed / **-oad** 62
elbows / **-ows** 85
elderberry / **-erry** 42
electric / **-ick** 46
electron / **-on** 68
elope / **-ope** 75
elsewhere / **-air** 15
e-mail / **-ale** 14
embark / **-ark** 22
embrace / **-ace** 9
embraced / **-aced** 9
embroil / **-oil** 65
emphasis / **-iss** 58
empire / **-ire** 57
employ / **-oy** 86
enchants / **-ance** 19
enclose / **-ows** 85
encore / **-ore** 76
encores / **-ores** 77
end / **-end** 41
engineer / **-ear** 31
enjoy / **-oy** 86
enjoys / **-oise** 66
enormous / **-us** 96
enough / **-uff** 89
enrage / **-age** 13
enrolled / **-old** 66
enthuse / **-use** 96
entrance / **-ance** 19
envelope / **-ope** 75
envious / **-us** 96
enzyme / **-ime** 54
epilogue / **-og** 65
episode / **-oad** 62
equator / **-ator** 26
erase / **-aze** 28
escalator / **-ator** 26
escapade / **-ade** 12
escape / **-ape** 21
essay / **-ay** 27
essays / **-aze** 28
estate / **-ate** 25
estimate / **-ate** 25
evade / **-ade** 12
evaporate / **-ate** 25
eve / **-eve** 44
event / **-ent** 41
evergreen / **-een** 37
evermore / **-ore** 76
everyone / **-un** 92
everything / **-ing** 56
everywhere / **-air** 15
ewe / **-oo** 70
exact / **-act** 11
exaggerate / **-ate** 25
exam / **-am** 17
exasperate / **-ate** 25
excavate / **-ate** 25
exceed / **-eed** 36
excel / **-ell** 39
except / **-ept** 42
excess / **-ess** 42
exciting / **-ing** 56
exclaim / **-ame** 18
exclude / **-ude** 88
excuse / **-oose** 74
excuse / **-use** 96
execute / **-ute** 98
exercise / **-ies** 49
exhale / **-ale** 14
expand / **-and** 19
expect / **-ect** 34
expel / **-ell** 39
expense / **-ence** 40
experiment / **-ent** 41
expert / **-urt** 96
explain / **-ane** 20
explode / **-oad** 62
explore / **-ore** 76
explored / **-oard** 62
explores / **-ores** 77
export / **-ort** 79
expose / **-ows** 85
express / **-ess** 42
expressed / **-est** 43
extend / **-end** 41
extract / **-act** 11
extreme / **-eam** 30
eye / **-i** 45
eyeball / **-all** 17
eyebrow / **-ow** 83
eyed / **-ide** 48
eyelash / **-ash** 23
eyelid / **-id** 47
eyesight / **-ight** 51
eyesore / **-ore** 76
eyesores / **-ores** 77

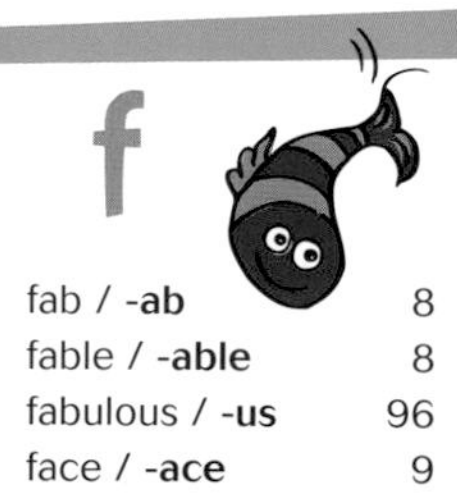

fab / **-ab** 8
fable / **-able** 8
fabulous / **-us** 96
face / **-ace** 9

faced / **-aced** 9
fact / **-act** 11
fad / **-ad** 12
fade / **-ade** 12
fail / **-ale** 14
fair / **-air** 15
fairground / **-ound** 82
fairy / **-airy** 16
fairyland / **-and** 19
fairytale / **-ale** 14
faithful / **-ul** 90
fake / **-ake** 16
fall / **-all** 17
falsehood / **-ood** 72
fame / **-ame** 18
famous / **-us** 96
fan / **-an** 18
fanfare / **-air** 15
fang / **-ang** 20
fanned / **-and** 19
fantastic / **-ick** 46
far / **-a** 8
fare / **-air** 15
farewell / **-ell** 39
farm / **-arm** 23
farming / **-ing** 56
farmyard / **-ard** 22
fascinate / **-ate** 25
fast / **-ast** 24
fat / **-at** 24
fate / **-ate** 25
fatherhood / **-ood** 72
fatter / **-atter** 26
faun / **-orn** 78
fax / **-acks** 11
faze / **-aze** 28
fear / **-ear** 31
fearful / **-ul** 90
feast / **-east** 32
feat / **-eat** 32
featherweight / **-ate** 25
fed / **-ed** 35
fee fie fo fum / **-um** 90
fee / **-e** 29
feed / **-eed** 36
feel / **-eal** 30
fees / **-ees** 38
feet / **-eat** 32
fell / **-ell** 39
fellow / **-ello** 39
felt / **-elt** 40
female / **-ale** 14
fen / **-en** 40
fence / **-ence** 40
fender / **-ender** 41
fern / **-urn** 94
ferry / **-erry** 42
ferryboat / **-oat** 63
festoon / **-oon** 73
fetch / **-etch** 44
fête / **-ate** 25
few / **-oo** 70
fiancé / **-ay** 27
fiancée / **-ay** 27
fib / **-ib** 46
fiddle / **-iddle** 47
fiddle-de-dee / **-e** 29
fiddlesticks / **-icks** 47
fidget / **-it** 59
fifteen / **-een** 37
fig / **-ig** 50
fight / **-ight** 51
figurehead / **-ed** 35
file / **-ile** 52
filed / **-ild** 52
fill / **-ill** 52
filmset / **-et** 44
fin / **-in** 54
find / **-ind** 55
fine / **-ine** 55
fingernail / **-ale** 14
fingerprint / **-int** 57
fingertip / **-ip** 57
fiord / **-oard** 62
fir / **-ur** 94
fire brigade / **-ade** 12
fire / **-ire** 57
fireball / **-all** 17
firebird / **-urred** 95
firebreak / **-ake** 16
fireflies / **-ies** 49
firefly / **-i** 45
fireguard / **-ard** 22
firelight / **-ight** 51
fireplace / **-ace** 9
fireside / **-ide** 48
firewood / **-ood** 72
firework / **-urk** 94
fish / **-ish** 58
fishbone / **-one** 69
fishbowl / **-ole** 67
fishcake / **-ake** 16
fishing / **-ing** 56
fishnet / **-et** 44
fishpond / **-ond** 69
fist / **-ist** 58
fistfight / **-ight** 51
fisticuff / **-uff** 89
fit / **-it** 59
fitter / **-itter** 60
five / **-ive** 60
fix / **-icks** 47
fizz / **-is** 58
flab / **-ab** 8
flabby / **-abby** 8
flag / **-ag** 13
flagpole / **-ole** 67
flair / **-air** 15
flake / **-ake** 16
flame / **-ame** 18
flamingo / **-o** 61
flamingos / **-ows** 85
flan / **-an** 18
flank / **-ank** 21
flap / **-ap** 21
flapjack / **-ack** 10
flapjacks / **-acks** 11
flare / **-air** 15
flash / **-ash** 23
flashback / **-ack** 10
flashlight / **-ight** 51
flask / **-ask** 23
flat / **-at** 24
flatter / **-atter** 26
flaw / **-ore** 76
flaws / **-ores** 77
flea / **-e** 29
fleabite / **-ight** 51
fleas / **-ees** 38
fleck / **-eck** 33
flecked / **-ect** 34
flecks / **-ecks** 34
fled / **-ed** 35
flee / **-e** 29
fleece / **-eece** 36
flees / **-ees** 38
fleet / **-eat** 32
flesh / **-esh** 42
flew / **-oo** 70
flex / **-ecks** 34
flick / **-ick** 46
flicks / **-icks** 47
flies / **-ies** 49
flight / **-ight** 51
flinch / **-inch** 55
fling / **-ing** 56
flint / **-int** 57
flip / **-ip** 57
flip-flop / **-op** 75
flirt / **-urt** 96
flit / **-it** 59
float / **-oat** 63
flock / **-ock** 64
flocks / **-ocks** 64
floe / **-o** 61
flog / **-og** 65
flood / **-ud** 88
floodlight / **-ight** 51
floor / **-ore** 76
floorboard / **-oard** 62
floors / **-ores** 77
flop / **-op** 75
floss / **-oss** 80
flour / **-ower** 84
flow / **-o** 61
flowed / **-oad** 62
flower / **-ower** 84
flowerbed / **-ed** 35
flowerpot / **-ot** 81
flown / **-one** 69
flows / **-ows** 85
flu / **-oo** 71
flue / **-oo** 71
fluff / **-uff** 89
flung / **-ung** 92
flunk / **-unk** 93
flush / **-ush** 97
flute / **-ute** 98
flutter / **-utter** 98
fly / **-i** 45
foal / **-ole** 67
foam / **-ome** 68
foe / **-o** 61
foes / **-ows** 85
fog / **-og** 65
foghorn / **-orn** 78
foglamp / **-amp** 18
foil / **-oil** 65
foist / **-oist** 66
fold / **-old** 66
folk / **-oke** 66
folklore / **-ore** 76
fond / **-ond** 69
fondue / **-oo** 71
food / **-ude** 88
fool / **-ool** 72
foot / **-oot** 74
football / **-all** 17
footbridge / **-idge** 49
foothold / **-old** 66
footloose / **-oose** 74
footprint / **-int** 57

footsore / **-ore** 76
footstool / **-ool** 72
footwear / **-air** 15
for / **-ore** 76
forbid / **-id** 47
force / **-orse** 79
ford / **-oard** 62
forecast / **-ast** 24
forecourt / **-ort** 79
foreground / **-ound** 82
forehand / **-and** 19
forehead / **-ed** 35
foreseen / **-een** 37
forevermore / **-ore** 76
forgave / **-ave** 27
forget / **-et** 44
forget-me-not / **-ot** 81
forgot / **-ot** 81
fork / **-ork** 78
forlorn / **-orn** 78
form / **-orm** 78
fort / **-ort** 79
forthright / **-ight** 51
fortnight / **-ight** 51
fortune / **-oon** 73
fought / **-ort** 79
foul / **-owl** 84
found / **-ound** 82
four / **-ore** 76
fourteen / **-een** 37
fowl / **-owl** 84
fox / **-ocks** 64
foxhound / **-ound** 82
fragile / **-ile** 52
fragment / **-ent** 41
frail / **-ale** 14
frame / **-ame** 18
framework / **-urk** 94
France / **-ance** 19
frank / **-ank** 21
frantic / **-antic** 21
fraught / **-ort** 79
fray / **-ay** 27
frayed / **-ade** 12
frays / **-aze** 28
freak / **-eek** 37
free / **-e** 29
freed / **-eed** 36
freedom / **-um** 90
freefall / **-all** 17
freehand / **-and** 19
freelance / **-ance** 19
frees / **-ees** 38
freestyle / **-ile** 52
freewheel / **-eal** 30
freewheeling / **-ing** 56
freeze / **-ees** 38
freight / **-ate** 25
French / **-ench** 40
fresh / **-esh** 42
fret / **-et** 44
Friday / **-ay** 27
fridge / **-idge** 49
fried / **-ide** 48
friend / **-end** 41
friendship / **-ip** 57
fries / **-ies** 49
fright / **-ight** 51
frill / **-ill** 52
frilly / **-illy** 53
fringe / **-inge** 56
fritter / **-itter** 60
frizz / **-is** 58
frock / **-ock** 64
frog / **-og** 65
frogmarch / **-arch** 22
frogspawn / **-orn** 78
front / **-unt** 93
frontier / **-ear** 31
frostbite / **-ight** 51
frown / **-own** 84
frowned / **-ound** 82
froze / **-ows** 85
fruit / **-ute** 98
fruitcake / **-ake** 16
frump / **-ump** 91
frustrate / **-ate** 25
fry / **-i** 45
fudge / **-udge** 89
fuel / **-ool** 72
fulfil / **-ill** 52
full / **-ul** 90
fumble / **-umble** 91
fume / **-oom** 73
fun / **-un** 92
funfair / **-air** 15
funk / **-unk** 93
fur / **-ur** 94
furious / **-us** 96
furrows / **-ows** 85
fuse / **-use** 96
fuss / **-us** 96
fussed / **-ust** 97
fusspot / **-ot** 81
fuzz / **-uzz** 98

g

gabble / **-abble** 8
gadget / **-it** 59
gag / **-ag** 13
gaga / **-a** 8
gale / **-ale** 14
galley / **-alley** 17
galore / **-ore** 76
game / **-ame** 18
gang / **-ang** 20
gangplank / **-ank** 21
gangway / **-ay** 27
gap / **-ap** 21
gape / **-ape** 21
gargoyle / **-oil** 65
garlic / **-ick** 46
gash / **-ash** 23
gasp / **-asp** 23
gate / **-ate** 25
gatecrash / **-ash** 23
gatepost / **-ost** 80
gauze / **-ores** 77
gave / **-ave** 27
gawk / **-ork** 78
gaze / **-aze** 28
gear / **-ear** 31
gearbox / **-ocks** 64
gel / **-ell** 39
gem / **-em** 40
gender / **-ender** 41
gene / **-een** 37
genie / **-e** 29
genius / **-us** 96
germinate / **-ate** 25
get / **-et** 44
ghost / **-ost** 80
ghostlike / **-ike** 51
ghoul / **-ool** 72
gift / **-ift** 50
gig / **-ig** 50
gigantic / **-antic** 21
giggle / **-iggle** 50
gill / **-ill** 52
gimmick / **-ick** 46
gimmicks / **-icks** 47
gingerbread / **-ed** 35
giraffe / **-arf** 22
girl / **-url** 94
girlfriend / **-end** 41
gist / **-ist** 58
glad / **-ad** 12
glade / **-ade** 12
glance / **-ance** 19
gland / **-and** 19
glare / **-air** 15
glass / **-ass** 24
glaze / **-aze** 28
gleam / **-eam** 30
glean / **-een** 37
glee / **-e** 29
glen / **-en** 40
glide / **-ide** 48
glint / **-int** 57
glitch / **-itch** 60
glitter / **-itter** 60
gloat / **-oat** 63
globe / **-obe** 64
globule / **-ool** 72
gloom / **-oom** 73
glorious / **-us** 96
gloss / **-oss** 80
glow / **-o** 61
glowed / **-oad** 62
glower / **-ower** 84
glows / **-ows** 85
glue / **-oo** 71
glued / **-ude** 88
glug / **-ug** 89
glum / **-um** 90
glut / **-ut** 97
gnash / **-ash** 23
gnat / **-at** 24
gnaw / **-ore** 76
gnaws / **-ores** 77
gnome / **-ome** 68
gnu / **-oo** 71
go / **-o** 61
goad / **-oad** 62
goal / **-ole** 67
goalpost / **-ost** 80
goat / **-oat** 63
goatherd / **-urred** 95
gobble / **-obble** 63
goblin / **-in** 54
god / **-od** 65
godchild / **-ild** 52
godson / **-un** 92
goes / **-ows** 85
go-kart / **-art** 23
gold / **-old** 66
goldfish / **-ish** 58
gondolier / **-ear** 31
gone / **-on** 68
gong / **-ong** 69

goo / **-oo** 70
good / **-ood** 72
goodbye / **-i** 45
goodwill / **-ill** 52
goose / **-oose** 74
gooseberry / **-erry** 42
goosebump / **-ump** 91
gooseflesh / **-esh** 42
gore / **-ore** 76
gores / **-ores** 77
gorgeous / **-us** 96
gosh / **-osh** 80
gossip / **-ip** 57
got / **-ot** 81
gown / **-own** 84
gowned / **-ound** 82
grab / **-ab** 8
grace / **-ace** 9
graced / **-aced** 9
graceful / **-ul** 90
grade / **-ade** 12
graffiti / **-e** 29
graft / **-aft** 13
grain / **-ane** 20
gram / **-am** 17
gran / **-an** 18
grand / **-and** 19
granddad / **-ad** 12
grandma / **-a** 8
grandpa / **-a** 8
grandson / **-un** 92
grandstand / **-and** 19
grants / **-ance** 19
grape / **-ape** 21
grapefruit / **-ute** 98
grapevine / **-ine** 55
graph / **-arf** 22
grasp / **-asp** 23
grass / **-ass** 24
grassed / **-ast** 24
grassland / **-and** 19
grate / **-ate** 25
grater / **-ator** 26
gratitude / **-ude** 88
grave / **-ave** 27
graveyard / **-ard** 22
graze / **-aze** 28
grease / **-eece** 36
greased / **-east** 32
Greece / **-eece** 36
greed / **-eed** 36
Greek / **-eek** 37
green / **-een** 37
greenfly / **-i** 45
greet / **-eat** 32
gremlin / **-in** 54
grenade / **-ade** 12
grew / **-oo** 70
grey / **-ay** 27
greyhound / **-ound** 82
grid / **-id** 47
griddle / **-iddle** 47
gridlock / **-ock** 64
gridlocks / **-ocks** 64
grief / **-eaf** 30
grieve / **-eve** 44
grill / **-ill** 52
grim / **-im** 53
grime / **-ime** 54
grin / **-in** 54
grind / **-ind** 55
grip / **-ip** 57
gripe / **-ipe** 57
grit / **-it** 59
groan / **-one** 69
grog / **-og** 65
groin / **-oin** 65
groom / **-oom** 73
grope / **-ope** 75
grouch / **-ouch** 81
ground / **-ound** 82
groundsheet / **-eat** 32
group / **-oop** 74
grouse / **-ouse** 83
grow / **-o** 61
growl / **-owl** 84
grown / **-one** 69
grows / **-ows** 85
grub / **-ub** 87
grudge / **-udge** 89
gruesome / **-um** 90
gruff / **-uff** 89
grumble / **-umble** 91
grunt / **-unt** 93
guarantee / **-e** 29
guaranteed / **-eed** 36
guarantees / **-ees** 38
guard / **-ard** 22
guess / **-ess** 42
guessed / **-est** 43
guesswork / **-urk** 94
guest / **-est** 43
guffaw / **-ore** 76
guffaws / **-ores** 77
guide / **-ide** 48
guideline / **-ine** 55
guillotine / **-een** 37
guilt / **-ilt** 53
guise / **-ies** 49
guitar / **-a** 8
gum / **-um** 90
gun / **-un** 92
gunfire / **-ire** 57
gunpoint / **-oint** 65
gunshot / **-ot** 81
guru / **-oo** 71
gush / **-ush** 97
gust / **-ust** 97
gusto / **-o** 61
gut / **-ut** 97
gutter / **-utter** 98
guttersnipe / **-ipe** 57
guy / **-i** 45
guzzle / **-uzzle** 98
gym / **-im** 53
gymnastics / **-icks** 47
gyroscope / **-ope** 75

h

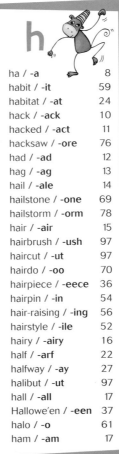

ha / **-a** 8
habit / **-it** 59
habitat / **-at** 24
hack / **-ack** 10
hacked / **-act** 11
hacksaw / **-ore** 76
had / **-ad** 12
hag / **-ag** 13
hail / **-ale** 14
hailstone / **-one** 69
hailstorm / **-orm** 78
hair / **-air** 15
hairbrush / **-ush** 97
haircut / **-ut** 97
hairdo / **-oo** 70
hairpiece / **-eece** 36
hairpin / **-in** 54
hair-raising / **-ing** 56
hairstyle / **-ile** 52
hairy / **-airy** 16
half / **-arf** 22
halfway / **-ay** 27
halibut / **-ut** 97
hall / **-all** 17
Hallowe'en / **-een** 37
halo / **-o** 61
ham / **-am** 17
hamper / **-amper** 18
hand / **-and** 19
handbag / **-ag** 13
handbook / **-ook** 72
handbrake / **-ake** 16
handcuff / **-uff** 89
handful / **-ul** 90
handicap / **-ap** 21
handiwork / **-urk** 95
handkerchief / **-eaf** 30
handlebar / **-a** 8
handmade / **-ade** 12
handset / **-et** 44
handshake / **-ake** 16
handstand / **-and** 19
handyman / **-an** 18
hang / **-ang** 20
hard / **-ard** 22
hardhat / **-at** 24
hardship / **-ip** 57
hardware / **-air** 15
hare / **-air** 15
hark / **-ark** 22
harm / **-arm** 23
harmful / **-ul** 90
harpoon / **-oon** 73
harpsichord / **-oard** 62
hash / **-ash** 23
haste / **-aced** 9
hat / **-at** 24
hatch / **-atch** 24
hate / **-ate** 25
haul / **-all** 17
hawk / **-ork** 78
hawthorn / **-orn** 78
hay / **-ay** 27
hayfork / **-ork** 78
haystack / **-ack** 10
haystacks / **-acks** 11
haywire / **-ire** 57
haze / **-aze** 28
hazelnut / **-ut** 97
he / **-e** 29
head / **-ed** 35
headache / **-ake** 16
headdress / **-ess** 42
headlight / **-ight** 51
headline / **-ine** 55
headlong / **-ong** 69
headset / **-et** 44
headscarf / **-arf** 22
headstand / **-and** 19
headstrong / **-ong** 69

heal / **-eal** 30
heap / **-eep** 38
hear / **-ear** 31
heard / **-urred** 95
hearing / **-ing** 56
heart / **-art** 23
heartache / **-ake** 16
heartbeat / **-eat** 32
heartbreak / **-ake** 16
heartfelt / **-elt** 40
heat / **-eat** 32
heater / **-eater** 33
heatwave / **-ave** 27
heave / **-eve** 44
heavyweight / **-ate** 25
hectic / **-ick** 46
hedge / **-edge** 35
hedgehog / **-og** 65
hedgerow / **-o** 61
hedgerows / **-ows** 85
heed / **-eed** 36
heel / **-eal** 30
height / **-ight** 51
heir / **-air** 15
heirloom / **-oom** 73
heliport / **-ort** 79
hell / **-ell** 39
hello / **-o** 61
hello / **-ello** 39
helmet / **-it** 59
help / **-elp** 39
helpful / **-ul** 90
helpless / **-ess** 42
hem / **-em** 40
hemisphere / **-ear** 31
hen / **-en** 40
henpecked / **-ect** 34
henpecks / **-ecks** 34
her / **-ur** 94
herbivore / **-ore** 76
herbivores / **-ores** 77
herd / **-urred** 95
here / **-ear** 31
hero / **-o** 61
hesitate / **-ate** 25
hey / **-ay** 27
hi / **-i** 45
hibernate / **-ate** 25
hic / **-ick** 46
hiccup / **-up** 93
hid / **-id** 47
hide / **-ide** 48
hideous / **-us** 96
hideout / **-out** 83
hi-fi / **-i** 45
high / **-i** 45
highchair / **-air** 15
highlight / **-ight** 51
highs / **-ies** 49
high-tech / **-eck** 33
highway / **-ay** 27
highwayman / **-an** 18
hijack / **-ack** 10
hijacked / **-act** 11
hijacks / **-acks** 11
hike / **-ike** 51
hilarious / **-us** 96
hill / **-ill** 52
hillside / **-ide** 48
hilltop / **-op** 75
hilly / **-illy** 53
hilt / **-ilt** 53
him / **-im** 53
Hindu / **-oo** 71
hinge / **-inge** 56
hint / **-int** 57
hip / **-ip** 57
hippo / **-o** 61
hippopotamus / **-us** 96
hippos / **-ows** 85
hire / **-ire** 57
his / **-is** 58
hissed / **-ist** 58
historic / **-ick** 46
hit / **-it** 59
hitch / **-itch** 60
hitchhike / **-ike** 51
hive / **-ive** 60
hoard / **-oard** 62
hoarse / **-orse** 79
hob / **-ob** 63
hobble / **-obble** 63
hobbyhorse / **-orse** 79
hobgoblin / **-in** 54
hobnob / **-ob** 63
hockey / **-ocky** 64
hocus-pocus / **-us** 96
hoe / **-o** 61
hoes / **-ows** 85
hog / **-og** 65
hoist / **-oist** 66
hold / **-old** 66
hole / **-ole** 67
holiday / **-ay** 27
holidays / **-aze** 28
hollyhocks / **-ocks** 64
Hollywood / **-ood** 72
hologram / **-am** 17
home / **-ome** 68
homemade / **-ade** 12
homesick / **-ick** 46
homework / **-urk** 94
honey / **-e** 29
honeybee / **-e** 29
honeybees / **-ees** 38
honeycomb / **-ome** 68
honeymoon / **-oon** 73
honeysuckle / **-uckle** 88
Hong Kong / **-ong** 69
hood / **-ood** 72
hoodwink / **-ink** 56
hook / **-ook** 72
hoop / **-oop** 74
hoopla / **-a** 8
hooray / **-ay** 27
hoot / **-ute** 98
hop / **-op** 75
hope / **-ope** 75
hopeful / **-ul** 90
horde / **-oard** 62
horn / **-orn** 78
hornpipe / **-ipe** 57
horoscope / **-ope** 75
horrendous / **-us** 96
horrific / **-ick** 46
horrified / **-ide** 48
horrifies / **-ies** 49
horrify / **-i** 45
horse / **-orse** 79
horseback / **-ack** 10
horsebox / **-ocks** 64
horsefly / **-i** 45
horseplay / **-ay** 27
horsepower / **-ower** 84
horseshoe / **-oo** 70
hose / **-ows** 85
host / **-ost** 80
hostile / **-ile** 52
hot / **-ot** 81
hotel / **-ell** 39
hotfoot / **-oot** 74
hothead / **-ed** 35
hothouse / **-ouse** 83
hound / **-ound** 82
hour / **-ower** 84
house / **-ouse** 83
houseboat / **-oat** 63
housebound / **-ound** 82
household / **-old** 66
houseroom / **-oom** 73
hovercraft / **-aft** 13
how / **-ow** 83
howl / **-owl** 84
hub / **-ub** 87
hubbub / **-ub** 87
hubcap / **-ap** 21
huddle / **-uddle** 88
hue / **-oo** 71
huff / **-uff** 89
hug / **-ug** 89
hullaballoo / **-oo** 70
hum / **-um** 90
humane / **-ane** 20
humankind / **-ind** 55
humble / **-umble** 91
humbug / **-ug** 89
humdrum / **-um** 90
humid / **-id** 47
hummingbird / **-urred** 95
hump / **-ump** 91
humpback / **-ack** 10
humpbacked / **-act** 11
hunch / **-unch** 92
hunchback / **-ack** 10
hunchbacked / **-act** 11
hung / **-ung** 92
hunt / **-unt** 93
hurl / **-url** 94
hurt / **-urt** 96
hurtful / **-ul** 90
hush / **-ush** 97
husk / **-usk** 97
hut / **-ut** 97
hutch / **-uch** 87
hydrofoil / **-oil** 65
hygiene / **-een** 37
hymn / **-im** 53
hype / **-ipe** 57
hypnotize / **-ies** 49
hysterics / **-icks** 47

i

I / **-i** 45
ice / **-ice** 46
icebound / **-ound** 82
icecap / **-ap** 21
icepack / **-ack** 10
icon / **-on** 68
ID / **-e** 29

ideal / **-eal** 30
idolize / **-ies** 49
if / **-iff** 49
igloo / **-oo** 70
ignite / **-ight** 51
ignore / **-ore** 76
ignored / **-oard** 62
ignores / **-ores** 77
ill / **-ill** 52
ill-starred / **-ard** 22
illustrate / **-ate** 25
illustrator / **-ator** 26
imbecile / **-eal** 30
imitate / **-ate** 25
immense / **-ence** 40
immerse / **-urse** 95
impact / **-act** 11
impale / **-ale** 14
impress / **-ess** 42
impressed / **-est** 43
in / **-in** 54
incense / **-ence** 40
inch / **-inch** 55
include / **-ude** 88
incorrect / **-ect** 34
increase / **-eece** 36
increased / **-east** 32
incubate / **-ate** 25
incubator / **-ator** 26
indeed / **-eed** 36
index / **-ecks** 34
indicate / **-ate** 25
indigo / **-o** 61
indoor / **-ore** 76
indoors / **-ores** 77
induce / **-oose** 74
inept / **-ept** 42
infect / **-ect** 34
inferno / **-o** 61
infest / **-est** 43
info / **-o** 61
inform / **-orm** 78
infrared / **-ed** 35
ingenious / **-us** 96
inhabit / **-it** 59
inhale / **-ale** 14
inherit / **-it** 59
inject / **-ect** 34
ink / **-ink** 56
innermost / **-ost** 80
input / **-oot** 74
insane / **-ane** 20
insect / **-ect** 34
inside / **-ide** 48
insight / **-ight** 51
insincere / **-ear** 31
insist / **-ist** 58
insole / **-ole** 67
insomniac / **-ack** 10
inspect / **-ect** 34
inspire / **-ire** 57
instead / **-ed** 35
insulate / **-ate** 25
intend / **-end** 41
intercept / **-ept** 42
interlaced / **-aced** 9
Internet / **-et** 44
interrogate / **-ate** 25
interview / **-oo** 70
interviewed / **-ude** 88
interviews / **-use** 96
introduce / **-oose** 74
intrude / **-ude** 88
invade / **-ade** 12
invalid / **-id** 47
invent / **-ent** 41
invest / **-est** 43
investigate / **-ate** 25
invite / **-ight** 51
irate / **-ate** 25
irk / **-urk** 94
ironclad / **-ad** 12
irritate / **-ate** 25
is / **-is** 58
isle / **-ile** 52
IT / **-e** 29
it / **-it** 59
itch / **-itch** 60
I've / **-ive** 60

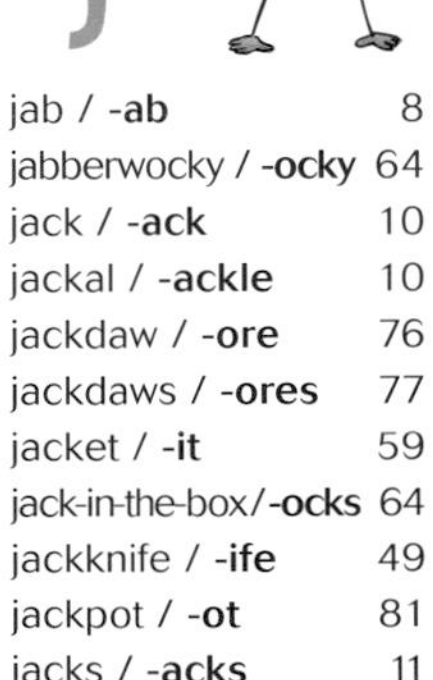

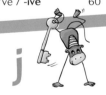

jab / **-ab** 8
jabberwocky / **-ocky** 64
jack / **-ack** 10
jackal / **-ackle** 10
jackdaw / **-ore** 76
jackdaws / **-ores** 77
jacket / **-it** 59
jack-in-the-box/**-ocks** 64
jackknife / **-ife** 49
jackpot / **-ot** 81
jacks / **-acks** 11
jade / **-ade** 12
jaguar / **-a** 8
jail / **-ale** 14
jailbird / **-urred** 95
jailbreak / **-ake** 16
jam / **-am** 17
jamboree / **-e** 29
jamborees / **-ees** 38
jam-packed / **-act** 11
jangle / **-angle** 20
Japan / **-an** 18
Japanese / **-ees** 38
jar / **-a** 8
javelin / **-in** 54
jaw / **-ore** 76
jawbone / **-one** 69
jaws / **-ores** 77
jealous / **-us** 96
jeep / **-eep** 38
jeer / **-ear** 31
jellyfish / **-ish** 58
jerk / **-urk** 94
jest / **-est** 43
jet / **-et** 44
jig / **-ig** 50
jiggle / **-iggle** 50
jigsaw / **-ore** 76
jigsaws / **-ores** 77
jilt / **-ilt** 53
jive / **-ive** 60
job / **-ob** 63
jockey / **-ocky** 64
jog / **-og** 65
join / **-oin** 65
joint / **-oint** 65
joist / **-oist** 66
joke / **-oke** 66
jolt / **-olt** 67
jot / **-ot** 81
joy / **-oy** 86
joyride / **-ide** 48
joys / **-oise** 66
jubilee / **-e** 29
judge / **-udge** 89
judo / **-o** 61
jug / **-ug** 89
juggernaut / **-ort** 79
juice / **-oose** 74
July / **-i** 45
jumble / **-umble** 91
jump / **-ump** 91
June / **-oon** 73
junk / **-unk** 93
just / **-ust** 97
jut / **-ut** 97

kaftan / **-an** 18
kaleidoscope / **-ope** 75
kangaroo / **-oo** 70
kangaroos / **-use** 96
kaput / **-oot** 74
kayak / **-ack** 10
kayaks / **-acks** 11
kazoo / **-oo** 70
kebab / **-ab** 8
keel / **-eal** 30
keen / **-een** 37
keep / **-eep** 38
keepsake / **-ake** 16
keg / **-eg** 39
kelp / **-elp** 39
kept / **-ept** 42
kerbstone / **-one** 69
ketchup / **-up** 93
kettle / **-ettle** 44
key / **-e** 29
keyboard / **-oard** 62
keyhole / **-ole** 67
keys / **-ees** 38
kick / **-ick** 46
kicks / **-icks** 47
kid / **-id** 47
kidnap / **-ap** 21
kill / **-ill** 52
killjoys / **-oise** 66
kilogram / **-am** 17
kilometre / **-eater** 33
kilt / **-ilt** 53
kin / **-in** 54
kind / **-ind** 55
kindness / **-ess** 42
king / **-ing** 56
kingdom / **-um** 90
kink / **-ink** 56
kip / **-ip** 57
kiss / **-iss** 58
kissed / **-ist** 58
kit / **-it** 59
kitchenette / **-et** 44
kite / **-ight** 51
knack / **-ack** 10

knead / **-eed** 36
knee / **-e** 29
kneecap / **-ap** 21
kneel / **-eal** 30
kneepad / **-ad** 12
knees / **-ees** 38
knelt / **-elt** 40
knew / **-oo** 70
knife / **-ife** 49
knight / **-ight** 51
knighthood / **-ood** 72
knit / **-it** 59
knitter / **-itter** 60
knob / **-ob** 63
knock / **-ock** 64
knockout / **-out** 83
knocks / **-ocks** 64
knockdown / **-own** 84
knock-kneed / **-eed** 36
knot / **-ot** 81
knotty / **-otty** 81
know / **-o** 61
knows / **-ows** 85
knuckle / **-uckle** 88
kumquat / **-ot** 81
kung fu / **-oo** 71

l

lab / **-ab** 8
label / **-able** 8
lace / **-ace** 9
laced / **-aced** 9
lack / **-ack** 10
lacked / **-act** 11
lacks / **-acks** 11
lad / **-ad** 12
ladybird / **-urred** 95
ladylike / **-ike** 51
lag / **-ag** 13
lagoon / **-oon** 73
laid / **-ade** 12
lair / **-air** 15
lake / **-ake** 16
lamb / **-am** 17
lambswool / **-ul** 90
lame / **-ame** 18
lament / **-ent** 41
lamp / **-amp** 18
lamplight / **-ight** 51
lamppost / **-ost** 80
lampshade / **-ade** 12
lance / **-ance** 19
land / **-and** 19
landlord / **-oard** 62
landmark / **-ark** 22
landscape / **-ape** 21
landslide / **-ide** 48
lane / **-ane** 20
lank / **-ank** 21
lap / **-ap** 21
lapel / **-ell** 39
laptop / **-op** 75
lard / **-ard** 22
lark / **-ark** 22
lash / **-ash** 23
last / **-ast** 24
latch / **-atch** 24
latchkey / **-e** 29
late / **-ate** 25
later / **-ator** 26
latitude / **-ude** 88
latter / **-atter** 26
laugh / **-arf** 22
laughed / **-aft** 13
launderette / **-et** 44
law / **-ore** 76
lawn / **-orn** 78
laws / **-ores** 77
lax / **-acks** 11
lay / **-ay** 27
layby / **-i** 45
lays / **-aze** 28
laze / **-aze** 28
lead / **-ed** 35
lead / **-eed** 36
leadership / **-ip** 57
leaf / **-eaf** 30
leak / **-eek** 37
lean / **-een** 37
leant / **-ent** 41
leap / **-eep** 38
leapfrog / **-og** 65
learn / **-urn** 94
lease / **-eece** 36
leased / **-east** 32
least / **-east** 32
leave / **-eve** 44
led / **-ed** 35
ledge / **-edge** 35
leek / **-eek** 37
leer / **-ear** 31
leg / **-eg** 39
lemon squeezy/**-easy** 32
lemonade / **-ade** 12
lend / **-end** 41
lender / **-ender** 41
lent / **-ent** 41
leotard / **-ard** 22
leprechaun / **-orn** 78
less / **-ess** 42
lest / **-est** 43
letdown / **-own** 84
lice / **-ice** 46
lick / **-ick** 46
licks / **-icks** 47
lid / **-id** 47
lie / **-i** 45
lied / **-ide** 48
lies / **-ies** 49
life / **-ife** 49
lifeblood / **-ud** 88
lifeboat / **-oat** 63
lifebuoy / **-oy** 86
lifeguard / **-ard** 22
lifeless / **-ess** 42
lifelike / **-ike** 51
lifespan / **-an** 18
lifestyle / **-ile** 52
lifetime / **-ime** 54
lift / **-ift** 50
light / **-ight** 51
lighthouse / **-ouse** 83
lightweight / **-ate** 25
like / **-ike** 51
likewise / **-ies** 49
lilo / **-o** 61
lilt / **-ilt** 53
lily / **-illy** 53
limb / **-im** 53
lime / **-ime** 54
limelight / **-ight** 51
limerick / **-ick** 46
limousine / **-een** 37
line / **-ine** 55
lined / **-ind** 55
link / **-ink** 56
lip / **-ip** 57
lipstick / **-ick** 46
liquid / **-id** 47
liquorice / **-iss** 58
list / **-ist** 58
lit / **-it** 59
litre / **-eater** 33
litter / **-itter** 60
litterbug / **-ug** 89
live / **-ive** 60
livelihood / **-ood** 72
liver / **-iver** 60
livestock / **-ock** 64
livid / **-id** 47
living / **-ing** 56
load / **-oad** 62
loam / **-ome** 68
loan / **-one** 69
lob / **-ob** 63
lock / **-ock** 64
locks / **-ocks** 64
log / **-og** 65
logo / **-o** 61
loin / **-oin** 65
lollipop / **-op** 75
lone / **-one** 69
loneliness / **-ess** 42
long / **-ong** 69
longbow / **-o** 61
longbows / **-ows** 85
longitude / **-ude** 88
loo / **-oo** 70
look / **-ook** 72
lookout / **-out** 83
loom / **-oom** 73
loop / **-oop** 74
loophole / **-ole** 67
loose / **-oose** 74
loot / **-ute** 98
lop / **-op** 75
lope / **-ope** 75
lord / **-oard** 62
lore / **-ore** 76
lose / **-use** 96
lot / **-ot** 81
lotion / **-otion** 81
loud / **-oud** 82
louse / **-ouse** 83
lout / **-out** 83
lovebird / **-urred** 95
low / **-o** 61
lowdown / **-own** 84
lows / **-ows** 85
loyal / **-oil** 65
luck / **-uck** 87
ludicrous / **-us** 96
ludo / **-o** 61
lug / **-ug** 89
lukewarm / **-orm** 78
lullabies / **-ies** 49
lullaby / **-i** 45
lumberjack / **-ack** 10

lump / **-ump** 91
lunatic / **-ick** 46
lunch / **-unch** 92
lunchbox / **-ocks** 64
lurk / **-urk** 94
lush / **-ush** 97
lute / **-ute** 98

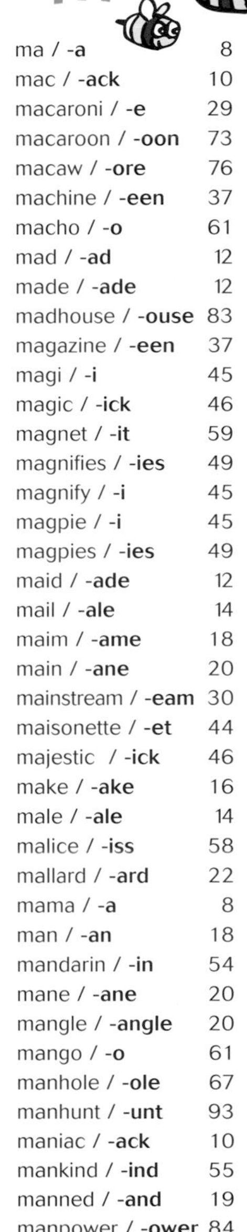

m

ma / **-a** 8
mac / **-ack** 10
macaroni / **-e** 29
macaroon / **-oon** 73
macaw / **-ore** 76
machine / **-een** 37
macho / **-o** 61
mad / **-ad** 12
made / **-ade** 12
madhouse / **-ouse** 83
magazine / **-een** 37
magi / **-i** 45
magic / **-ick** 46
magnet / **-it** 59
magnifies / **-ies** 49
magnify / **-i** 45
magpie / **-i** 45
magpies / **-ies** 49
maid / **-ade** 12
mail / **-ale** 14
maim / **-ame** 18
main / **-ane** 20
mainstream / **-eam** 30
maisonette / **-et** 44
majestic / **-ick** 46
make / **-ake** 16
male / **-ale** 14
malice / **-iss** 58
mallard / **-ard** 22
mama / **-a** 8
man / **-an** 18
mandarin / **-in** 54
mane / **-ane** 20
mangle / **-angle** 20
mango / **-o** 61
manhole / **-ole** 67
manhunt / **-unt** 93
maniac / **-ack** 10
mankind / **-ind** 55
manned / **-and** 19
manpower / **-ower** 84
mantelpiece / **-eece** 36
map / **-ap** 21
march / **-arch** 22
March / **-arch** 22
mare / **-air** 15
margarine / **-een** 37
margin / **-in** 54
marigold / **-old** 66
marine / **-een** 37
mark / **-ark** 22
marmalade / **-ade** 12
maroon / **-oon** 73
marquee / **-e** 29
marquees / **-ees** 38
marred / **-ard** 22
marrow / **-o** 61
marzipan / **-an** 18
mascot / **-ot** 81
mash / **-ash** 23
mask / **-ask** 23
mast / **-ast** 24
mastermind / **-ind** 55
masterpiece / **-eece** 36
mat / **-at** 24
matador / **-ore** 76
matadors / **-ores** 77
match / **-atch** 24
matchbox / **-ocks** 64
matchstick / **-ick** 46
matchsticks / **-icks** 47
mate / **-ate** 25
matrix / **-icks** 47
matter / **-atter** 26
mattress / **-ess** 42
maul / **-all** 17
max / **-acks** 11
maximum / **-um** 90
may / **-ay** 27
Mayflower / **-ower** 84
mayhem / **-em** 40
mayonnaise / **-aze** 28
maypole / **-ole** 67
maze / **-aze** 28
me / **-e** 29
meadow / **-o** 61
meadows / **-ows** 85
meal / **-eal** 30
mean / **-een** 37
meant / **-ent** 41
meantime / **-ime** 54
meanwhile / **-ile** 52
meat / **-eat** 32
meatball / **-all** 17
mechanic / **-ick** 46
meddlesome / **-um** 90
meditate / **-ate** 25
medium / **-um** 90
meek / **-eek** 37
meet / **-eat** 32
megabyte / **-ight** 51
megaphone / **-one** 69
mellow / **-ello** 39
melt / **-elt** 40
meltdown / **-own** 84
membership / **-ip** 57
memorize / **-ies** 49
men / **-en** 40
mend / **-end** 41
mentor / **-ore** 76
menu / **-oo** 71
meow / **-ow** 83
meowed / **-oud** 82
mere / **-ear** 31
meringue / **-ang** 20
mermaid / **-ade** 12
merrily / **-illy** 53
merry / **-erry** 42
mesh / **-esh** 42
mesmerize / **-ies** 49
mess / **-ess** 42
messed / **-est** 43
met / **-et** 44
metal / **-ettle** 44
metallic / **-ick** 46
metaphor / **-ore** 76
metaphors / **-ores** 77
meteor / **-ore** 76
meteorite / **-ight** 51
meteors / **-ores** 77
meter / **-eater** 33
metre / **-eater** 33
metro / **-o** 61
metronome / **-ome** 68
mettle / **-ettle** 44
mew / **-oo** 70
mewed / **-ude** 88
mice / **-ice** 46
microbe / **-obe** 64
microchip / **-ip** 57
microphone / **-one** 69
microscope / **-ope** 75
microwave / **-ave** 27
mid-air / **-air** 15
midday / **-ay** 27
middle / **-iddle** 47
midge / **-idge** 49
midnight / **-ight** 51
midweek / **-eek** 37
miffed / **-ift** 50
might / **-ight** 51
migrate / **-ate** 25
mild / **-ild** 52
mile / **-ile** 52
milkshake / **-ake** 16
mill / **-ill** 52
millennium / **-um** 90
milligram / **-am** 17
millilitre / **-eater** 33
millimetre / **-eater** 33
millionaire / **-air** 15
millipede / **-eed** 36
mime / **-ime** 54
mincemeat / **-eat** 32
mind / **-ind** 55
mine / **-ine** 55
minibus / **-us** 96
minicab / **-ab** 8
minim / **-im** 53
minimum / **-um** 90
miniskirt / **-urt** 96
mink / **-ink** 56
minnow / **-o** 61
Minotaur / **-ore** 76
mint / **-int** 57
minus / **-us** 96
minuscule / **-ool** 72
minute / **-ute** 98
misbehave / **-ave** 27
mischievous / **-us** 96
misdeed / **-eed** 36
mishap / **-ap** 21
misjudge / **-udge** 89
mislead / **-eed** 36
misled / **-ed** 35
mismatch / **-atch** 24
misplace / **-ace** 9
misplaced / **-aced** 9
misprint / **-int** 57
misread / **-eed** 36
miss / **-iss** 58
missed / **-ist** 58
missile / **-ile** 52
misspell / **-ell** 39
mist / **-ist** 58
mistake / **-ake** 16
mistletoe / **-o** 61
mistook / **-ook** 72
mistrust / **-ust** 97
misunderstand / **-and** 19

misunderstood / **-ood** 72
misuse / **-oose** 74
mite / **-ight** 51
mix / **-icks** 47
moan / **-one** 69
moat / **-oat** 63
mob / **-ob** 63
mobile / **-ile** 52
mobilize / **-ies** 49
mock / **-ock** 64
mockingbird / **-urred** 95
mocks / **-ocks** 64
modem / **-em** 40
moist / **-oist** 66
mole / **-ole** 67
molecule / **-ool** 72
molehill / **-ill** 52
Monday / **-ay** 27
money / **-e** 29
mongoose / **-oose** 74
monk / **-unk** 93
monkey / **-e** 29
monkeys / **-ees** 38
monologue / **-og** 65
monorail / **-ale** 14
monsoon / **-oon** 73
monstrous / **-us** 96
moo / **-oo** 70
mood / **-ude** 88
mooed / **-ude** 88
moon / **-oon** 73
moonbeam / **-eam** 30
moonlight / **-ight** 51
moonlit / **-it** 59
moonshine / **-ine** 55
moonstruck / **-uck** 87
moose / **-oose** 74
mop / **-op** 75
mope / **-ope** 75
moped / **-ed** 35
more / **-ore** 76
morn / **-orn** 78
morose / **-ose** 80
mosaic / **-ick** 46
moss / **-oss** 80
most / **-ost** 80
motel / **-ell** 39
motherhood / **-ood** 72
motif / **-eaf** 30
motion / **-otion** 81
motocross / **-oss** 80
motorbike / **-ike** 51
motorboat / **-oat** 63
motorway / **-ay** 27
mould / **-old** 66
mount / **-ount** 82
mountaineer / **-ear** 31
mourn / **-orn** 78
mousetrap / **-ap** 21
mouthful / **-ul** 90
mouthwash / **-osh** 80
mow / **-o** 61
mowed / **-oad** 62
mown / **-one** 69
mows / **-ows** 85
much / **-uch** 87
muck / **-uck** 87
mud / **-ud** 88
muddle / **-uddle** 88
mudguard / **-ard** 22
muffin / **-in** 54
mug / **-ug** 89
mugshot / **-ot** 81
mule / **-ool** 72
multiplied / **-ide** 48
multiplies / **-ies** 49
multiply / **-i** 45
mum / **-um** 90
mumble / **-umble** 91
mummy / **-ummy** 91
munch / **-unch** 92
muse / **-use** 96
museum / **-um** 90
mush / **-ush** 97
mushroom / **-oom** 73
music / **-ick** 46
musk / **-usk** 97
musketeer / **-ear** 31
must / **-ust** 97
mute / **-ute** 98
mutt / **-ut** 97
mutter / **-utter** 98
muzzle / **-uzzle** 98
my / **-i** 45
mysterious / **-us** 96
mystified / **-ide** 48
mystify / **-i** 45
mystique / **-eek** 37

n

nab / **-ab** 8
nag / **-ag** 13
nail / **-ale** 14
name / **-ame** 18
namesake / **-ake** 16
nan / **-an** 18
nap / **-ap** 21
nape / **-ape** 21
narrator / **-ator** 26
natter / **-atter** 26
natty / **-atty** 26
navigator / **-ator** 26
near / **-ear** 31
nearby / **-i** 45
neat / **-eat** 32
neater / **-eater** 33
neck / **-eck** 33
necks / **-ecks** 34
nectarine / **-een** 37
need / **-eed** 36
neglect / **-ect** 34
neigh / **-ay** 27
neighbourhood / **-ood** 72
neighed / **-ade** 12
neon / **-on** 68
nephew / **-oo** 70
Neptune / **-oon** 73
nerd / **-urred** 95
nervous / **-us** 96
nest / **-est** 43
net / **-et** 44
netball / **-all** 17
nettle / **-ettle** 44
network / **-urk** 94
neutron / **-on** 68
nevermore / **-ore** 76
New York / **-ork** 78
new / **-oo** 70
newborn / **-orn** 78
newfound / **-ound** 82
newlywed / **-ed** 35
news / **-use** 96
newsflash / **-ash** 23
newsprint / **-int** 57
newt / **-ute** 98
nibble / **-ibble** 46
nice / **-ice** 46
nickname / **-ame** 18
nicks / **-icks** 47
niece / **-eece** 36
niggle / **-iggle** 50
night / **-ight** 51
nightcap / **-ap** 21
nightdress / **-ess** 42
nightfall / **-all** 17
nightgown / **-own** 84
nightingale / **-ale** 14
nightmare / **-air** 15
nightwear / **-air** 15
nil / **-ill** 52
Nile / **-ile** 52
nincompoop / **-oop** 74
nine / **-ine** 55
nineteen / **-een** 37
nip / **-ip** 57
nit / **-it** 59
nitpick / **-ick** 46
no / **-o** 61
nod / **-od** 65
noise / **-oise** 66
nomad / **-ad** 12
none / **-un** 92
nonetheless / **-ess** 42
nonplussed / **-ust** 97
nonsense / **-ence** 40
non-slip / **-ip** 57
non-stick / **-ick** 46
nonstop / **-op** 75
nook / **-ook** 72
noon / **-oon** 73
noose / **-oose** 74
nor / **-ore** 76
Norse / **-orse** 79
northbound / **-ound** 82
northeast / **-east** 32
northwest / **-est** 43
nose / **-ows** 85
nosebleed / **-eed** 36
nosering / **-ing** 56
nosh / **-osh** 80
not / **-ot** 81
note / **-oat** 63
notebook / **-ook** 72
nothing / **-ing** 56
notion / **-otion** 81
nought / **-ort** 79
noun / **-own** 84
novice / **-iss** 58
now / **-ow** 83
nowadays / **-aze** 28
nowhere / **-air** 15
nude / **-ude** 88
nudge / **-udge** 89
nugget / **-it** 59
numb / **-um** 90
numerous / **-us** 96
nun / **-un** 92
nurse / **-urse** 95
nut / **-ut** 97

nutcase / -ace 9
nutmeg / -eg 39
nutshell / -ell 39
nutter / -utter 98
nuzzle / -uzzle 98
nylon / -on 68

O

oak / -oke 66
oar / -ore 76
oars / -ores 77
oatcake / -ake 16
oatmeal / -eal 30
obey / -ay 27
obeyed / -ade 12
object / -ect 34
oblique / -eek 37
oblong / -ong 69
oboe / -o 61
oboes / -ows 85
obsessed / -est 43
obvious / -us 96
occur / -ur 94
ocean / -otion 81
o'clock / -ock 64
octopus / -us 96
oddball / -all 17
ode / -oad 62
offence / -ence 40
offend / -end 41
offender / -ender 41
offhand / -and 19
office / -iss 58
offshoot / -ute 98
offside / -ide 48
offstage / -age 13
oil / -oil 65
okay / -ay 27
old / -old 66
omelette / -et 44
on / -on 68
one / -un 92
onslaught / -ort 79
ooze / -use 96
opaque / -ake 16
operate / -ate 25
operator / -ator 26
oppose / -ows 85
oppress / -ess 42
orangeade / -ade 12
orang-utan / -an 18
orbit / -it 59
ordeal / -eal 30
ore / -ore 76
organic / -ick 46
origin / -in 54
ornament / -ent 41
ostrich / -itch 60
ouch! / -ouch 81
ought / -ort 79
our / -ower 84
out / -out 83
outback / -ack 10
outboard / -oard 62
outbreak / -ake 16
outcast / -ast 24
outclass / -ass 24
outcome / -um 90
outcry / -i 45
outdone / -un 92
outdoor / -ore 76
outdoors / -ores 77
outermost / -ost 80
outfit / -it 59
outgrow / -o 61
outgrows / -ows 85
outlast / -ast 24
outlaw / -ore 76
outlaws / -ores 77
outline / -ine 55
outlined / -ind 55
outlook / -ook 72
outpaced / -aced 9
outpost / -ost 80
output / -oot 74
outrage / -age 13
outright / -ight 51
outshine / -ine 55
outside / -ide 48
outsize / -ies 49
outsmart / -art 23
outspread / -ed 35
outweighed / -ade 12
outwit / -it 59
overact / -act 11
overall / -all 17
overarm / -arm 23
overate / -ate 25
overboard / -oard 62
overcame / -ame 18
overcast / -ast 24
overcoat / -oat 63
overcome / -um 90
overcook / -ook 72
overcrowd / -oud 82
overdose / -ose 80
overdressed / -est 43
overdue / -oo 71
overeat / -eat 32
overexpose / -ows 85
overfed / -ed 35
overfill / -ill 52
overflow / -o 61
overflowed / -oad 62
overflows / -ows 85
overfull / -ul 90
overgrown / -one 69
overhang / -ang 20
overhaul / -all 17
overhead / -ed 35
overhear / -ear 31
overheard / -urred 95
overheat / -eat 32
overkill / -ill 52
overland / -and 19
overlap / -ap 21
overleaf / -eaf 30
overload / -oad 62
overlook / -ook 72
overnight / -ight 51
overpaid / -ade 12
overpower / -ower 84
overreact / -act 11
overripe / -ipe 57
overrule / -ool 72
overseas / -ees 38
oversee / -e 29
oversees / -ees 38
oversight / -ight 51
oversleep / -eep 38
overslept / -ept 42
overspend / -end 41
overspent / -ent 41
overstepped / -ept 42
overstuff / -uff 89
overtake / -ake 16
overthrows / -ows 85
overtime / -ime 54
overtook / -ook 72
overweight / -ate 25
overwork / -urk 94
ow! / -ow 83
owed / -oad 62
owl / -owl 84
own / -one 69
ox / -ocks 64
ozone / -one 69

P

pa / -a 8
pace / -ace 9
paced / -aced 9
Pacific / -ick 46
pack / -ack 10
packed / -act 11
packs / -acks 11
pact / -act 11
pad / -ad 12
padlock / -ock 64
padlocks / -ocks 64
page / -age 13
paid / -ade 12
pail / -ale 14
pain / -ane 20
paintbox / -ocks 64
paintbrush / -ush 97
pair / -air 15
pale / -ale 14
palindrome / -ome 68
pall / -all 17
pally / -alley 17
palm / -arm 23
pamper / -amper 18
pan / -an 18
Panama / -a 8
pancake / -ake 16
pane / -ane 20
pang / -ang 20
panic / -ick 46
pant / -ant 21
pantomime / -ime 54
papa / -a 8
paperback / -ack 10
paperboy / -oy 86
paperclip / -ip 57
paperweight / -ate 25
papoose / -oose 74
papyrus / -us 96
parachute / -ute 98
parade / -ade 12
paradise / -ice 46
paradox / -ocks 64
paragraph / -arf 22

parakeet / **-eat** 32
parallel / **-ell** 39
parasite / **-ight** 51
paratroop / **-oop** 74
parch / **-arch** 22
Paris / **-iss** 58
park / **-ark** 22
paroled / **-old** 66
part / **-art** 23
pass / **-ass** 24
passed / **-ast** 24
passer-by / **-i** 45
passport / **-ort** 79
password / **-urred** 95
past / **-ast** 24
paste / **-aced** 9
pastime / **-ime** 54
pat / **-at** 24
pat-a-cake / **-ake** 16
patch / **-atch** 24
pâté / **-ay** 27
pathway / **-ay** 27
pathways / **-aze** 28
patio / **-o** 61
patrol / **-ole** 67
patrolled / **-old** 66
patter / **-atter** 26
patty / **-atty** 26
pause / **-ores** 77
pave / **-ave** 27
paw / **-ore** 76
pawn / **-orn** 78
pawpaw / **-ore** 76
pawpaws / **-ores** 77
paws / **-ores** 77
pay / **-ay** 27
pays / **-aze** 28
PC / **-e** 29
PE / **-e** 29
pea / **-e** 29
peace / **-eece** 36
peaceful / **-ul** 90
peacetime / **-ime** 54
peacock / **-ock** 64
peacocks / **-ocks** 64
peak / **-eek** 37
peal / **-eal** 30
peanut / **-ut** 97
peapod / **-od** 65
pear / **-air** 15
pearl / **-url** 94
peas / **-ees** 38
peat / **-eat** 32
peck / **-eck** 33
pecked / **-ect** 34
pecks / **-ecks** 34
pedantic / **-antic** 21
pedigree / **-e** 29
pedigrees / **-ees** 38
peek / **-eek** 37
peekaboo / **-oo** 70
peel / **-eal** 30
peep / **-eep** 38
peephole / **-ole** 67
peer / **-ear** 31
peg / **-eg** 39
Pekinese / **-ees** 38
pelt / **-elt** 40
pen / **-en** 40
pence / **-ence** 40
pendulum / **-um** 90
penguin / **-in** 54
penknife / **-ife** 49
pennypinch / **-inch** 55
peppercorn / **-orn** 78
peppermint / **-int** 57
per / **-ur** 94
perceive / **-eve** 44
perfect / **-ect** 34
perform / **-orm** 78
perfume / **-oom** 73
periscope / **-ope** 75
perish / **-ish** 58
perk / **-urk** 94
permit / **-it** 59
perplex / **-ecks** 34
persevere / **-ear** 31
perspire / **-ire** 57
persuade / **-ade** 12
pert / **-urt** 96
Peru / **-oo** 71
peruse / **-use** 96
pest / **-est** 43
pesticide / **-ide** 48
pet / **-et** 44
petal / **-ettle** 44
petrified / **-ide** 48
petrifies / **-ies** 49
petrify / **-i** 45
petticoat / **-oat** 63
pew / **-oo** 70
phase / **-aze** 28
phew / **-oo** 70
phial / **-ile** 52
phoenix / **-icks** 47
phone / **-one** 69
photo / **-o** 61
photograph / **-arf** 22
phrase / **-aze** 28
phut / **-ut** 97
piano / **-o** 61
pianos / **-ows** 85
piccolo / **-o** 61
pick / **-ick** 46
pickaxe / **-acks** 11
picks / **-icks** 47
picnic / **-ick** 46
picnics / **-icks** 47
pie / **-i** 45
piece / **-eece** 36
pieced / **-east** 32
pier / **-ear** 31
pies / **-ies** 49
pig / **-ig** 50
piggyback / **-ack** 10
piglet / **-it** 59
pigpen / **-en** 40
pigsties / **-ies** 49
pigsty / **-i** 45
pigswill / **-ill** 52
pigtail / **-ale** 14
pike / **-ike** 51
pile / **-ile** 52
piled / **-ild** 52
pilgrim / **-im** 53
pill / **-ill** 52
pillow / **-o** 61
pillowcase / **-ace** 9
pin / **-in** 54
pinafores / **-ores** 77
pinball / **-all** 17
pinch / **-inch** 55
pine / **-ine** 55
pined / **-ind** 55
ping / **-ing** 56
ping-pong / **-ong** 69
pinhead / **-ed** 35
pinhole / **-ole** 67
pink / **-ink** 56
pinpoint / **-oint** 65
pinprick / **-ick** 46
pinpricks / **-icks** 47
pinstripe / **-ipe** 57
pioneer / **-ear** 31
pip / **-ip** 57
pipe / **-ipe** 57
pipeline / **-ine** 55
pique / **-eek** 37
pirouette / **-et** 44
pit / **-it** 59
pitch / **-itch** 60
pitchfork / **-ork** 78
pitfall / **-all** 17
pitiful / **-ul** 90
pixie / **-e** 29
place / **-ace** 9
placed / **-aced** 9
plain / **-ane** 20
plan / **-an** 18
plane / **-ane** 20
plank / **-ank** 21
planned / **-and** 19
plants / **-ance** 19
plaque / **-ack** 10
plastic / **-ick** 46
plate / **-ate** 25
platform / **-orm** 78
platoon / **-oon** 73
platter / **-atter** 26
platypus / **-us** 96
play / **-ay** 27
playboy / **-oy** 86
played / **-ade** 12
playful / **-ul** 90
playground / **-ound** 82
playgroup / **-oop** 74
playmate / **-ate** 25
playpen / **-en** 40
playroom / **-oom** 73
plays / **-aze** 28
playschool / **-ool** 72
playtime / **-ime** 54
playwright / **-ight** 51
plea / **-e** 29
plead / **-eed** 36
pleas / **-ees** 38
please / **-ees** 38
pleat / **-eat** 32
plectrum / **-um** 90
pledge / **-edge** 35
plentiful / **-ul** 90
plight / **-ight** 51
plod / **-od** 65
plop / **-op** 75
plot / **-ot** 81
plough / **-ow** 83
ploy / **-oy** 86
ploys / **-oise** 66
pluck / **-uck** 87
plug / **-ug** 89
plum / **-um** 90
plumb / **-um** 90

plume / **-oom** 73
plump / **-ump** 91
plunder / **-under** 92
plus / **-us** 96
plush / **-ush** 97
plywood / **-ood** 72
pocket / **-it** 59
pocketknife / **-ife** 49
pod / **-od** 65
pogo / **-o** 61
point / **-oint** 65
poise / **-oise** 66
poke / **-oke** 66
pole / **-ole** 67
poleaxe / **-acks** 11
police / **-eece** 36
policed / **-east** 32
polite / **-ight** 51
polled / **-old** 66
pollute / **-ute** 98
ponchos / **-ows** 85
pond / **-ond** 69
pong / **-ong** 69
ponytail / **-ale** 14
pool / **-ool** 72
poor / **-ore** 76
pop / **-op** 75
popcorn / **-orn** 78
pope / **-ope** 75
porcupine / **-ine** 55
pore / **-ore** 76
pores / **-ores** 77
pork / **-ork** 78
porridge / **-idge** 49
port / **-ort** 79
portcullis / **-iss** 58
porthole / **-ole** 67
portrait / **-ate** 25
portrayed / **-ade** 12
pose / **-ows** 85
posh / **-osh** 80
posse / **-e** 29
possess / **-ess** 42
possessed / **-est** 43
post / **-ost** 80
postbag / **-ag** 13
postbox / **-ocks** 64
postcard / **-ard** 22
postcode / **-oad** 62
postmark / **-ark** 22
postpone / **-one** 69
pot / **-ot** 81
potato / **-o** 61
pothole / **-ole** 67
potion / **-otion** 81
potty / **-otty** 81
pouch / **-ouch** 81
pound / **-ound** 82
pour / **-ore** 76
pours / **-ores** 77
pout / **-out** 83
pow / **-ow** 83
power / **-ower** 84
powerboat / **-oat** 63
powerful / **-ul** 90
pow-wow / **-ow** 83
pox / **-ocks** 64
practice / **-iss** 58
prairie / **-airy** 16
praise / **-aze** 28
pram / **-am** 17
prance / **-ance** 19
prang / **-ang** 20
prank / **-ank** 21
prawn / **-orn** 78
pray / **-ay** 27
prayed / **-ade** 12
prays / **-aze** 28
precious / **-us** 96
precipice / **-iss** 58
precise / **-ice** 46
preen / **-een** 37
prefect / **-ect** 34
prefer / **-ur** 94
prehistoric / **-ick** 46
premiership / **-ip** 57
prepare / **-air** 15
present / **-ent** 41
press / **-ess** 42
pressed / **-est** 43
pretence / **-ence** 40
pretend / **-end** 41
prevent / **-ent** 41
prey / **-ay** 27
preyed / **-ade** 12
price / **-ice** 46
pricks / **-icks** 47
pride / **-ide** 48
prim / **-im** 53
primate / **-ate** 25
prime / **-ime** 54
primrose / **-ows** 85
princess / **-ess** 42
print / **-int** 57
prise / **-ies** 49
prize / **-ies** 49
probe / **-obe** 64
proceed / **-eed** 36
proclaim / **-ame** 18
prod / **-od** 65
produce / **-oose** 74
profile / **-ile** 52
profound / **-ound** 82
program / **-am** 17
progress / **-ess** 42
progressed / **-est** 43
prohibit / **-it** 59
project / **-ect** 34
prologue / **-og** 65
promote / **-oat** 63
prone / **-one** 69
prong / **-ong** 69
proofread / **-eed** 36
prop / **-op** 75
propel / **-ell** 39
propose / **-ows** 85
prose / **-ows** 85
protect / **-ect** 34
protest / **-est** 43
prototype / **-ipe** 57
proud / **-oud** 82
provoke / **-oke** 66
prow / **-ow** 83
prowl / **-owl** 84
prune / **-oon** 73
pry / **-i** 45
psalm / **-arm** 23
pseudonym / **-im** 53
pterosaur / **-ore** 76
pub / **-ub** 87
public / **-ick** 46
puck / **-uck** 87
pudding / **-ing** 56
puddle / **-uddle** 88
puff / **-uff** 89
puffin / **-in** 54
pull / **-ul** 90
pump / **-ump** 91
pumpkin / **-in** 54
pun / **-un** 92
punch / **-unch** 92
punchbag / **-ag** 13
punchline / **-ine** 55
punish / **-ish** 58
punk / **-unk** 93
punt / **-unt** 93
pup / **-up** 93
puppet / **-it** 59
puppeteer / **-ear** 31
purred / **-urred** 95
purse / **-urse** 95
pursue / **-oo** 71
pursued / **-ude** 88
pus / **-us** 96
pushchair / **-air** 15
pussycat / **-at** 24
pussyfoot / **-oot** 74
put / **-oot** 74
putt / **-ut** 97
putter / **-utter** 98
puzzle / **-uzzle** 98
pylon / **-on** 68
pyramid / **-id** 47

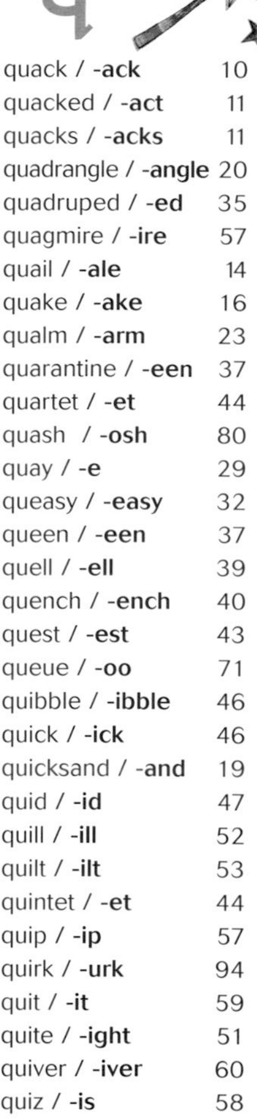

quack / **-ack** 10
quacked / **-act** 11
quacks / **-acks** 11
quadrangle / **-angle** 20
quadruped / **-ed** 35
quagmire / **-ire** 57
quail / **-ale** 14
quake / **-ake** 16
qualm / **-arm** 23
quarantine / **-een** 37
quartet / **-et** 44
quash / **-osh** 80
quay / **-e** 29
queasy / **-easy** 32
queen / **-een** 37
quell / **-ell** 39
quench / **-ench** 40
quest / **-est** 43
queue / **-oo** 71
quibble / **-ibble** 46
quick / **-ick** 46
quicksand / **-and** 19
quid / **-id** 47
quill / **-ill** 52
quilt / **-ilt** 53
quintet / **-et** 44
quip / **-ip** 57
quirk / **-urk** 94
quit / **-it** 59
quite / **-ight** 51
quiver / **-iver** 60
quiz / **-is** 58
quote / **-oat** 63

r

rabbi / -i 45
rabbit / -it 59
raccoon / -oon 73
race / -ace 9
racecourse / -orse 79
raced / -aced 9
racehorse / -orse 79
racetrack / -ack 10
racing / -ing 56
rack / -ack 10
racket / -it 59
racks / -acks 11
radar / -a 8
radiator / -ator 26
radio / -o 61
radios / -ows 85
radius / -us 96
raft / -aft 13
rag / -ag 13
rage / -age 13
raid / -ade 12
rail / -ale 14
railing / -ing 56
railway / -ay 27
railways / -aze 28
rain / -ane 20
rainbow / -o 61
rainbows / -ows 85
raincoat / -oat 63
raindrop / -op 75
rainfall / -all 17
rainstorm / -orm 78
rainswept / -ept 42
raise / -aze 28
rake / -ake 16
rally / -alley 17
ram / -am 17
ramp / -amp 18
rampage / -age 13
ramshackle / -ackle 10
ran / -an 18
rang / -ang 20
ransack / -ack 10
ransacked / -act 11
ransacks / -acks 11
rant / -ant 21
rap / -ap 21
rapid / -id 47
rare / -air 15
rash / -ash 23
rasp / -asp 23
raspberry / -erry 42
rat / -at 24
ratbag / -ag 13
rate / -ate 25
rattle / -attle 26
rattlesnake / -ake 16
ratty / -atty 26
raucous / -us 96
rave / -ave 27
ravenous / -us 96
ravine / -een 37
raw / -ore 76
ray / -ay 27
rays / -aze 28
raze / -aze 28
react / -act 11
read / -ed 35
read / -eed 36
readily / -illy 53
real / -eal 30
realize / -ies 49
reap / -eep 38
reappear / -ear 31
rear / -ear 31
rebel / -ell 39
reboot / -ute 98
rebut / -ut 97
recall / -all 17
recap / -ap 21
receive / -eve 44
recipe / -e 29
recite / -ight 51
reclaim / -ame 18
recluse / -oose 74
recognize / -ies 49
recoil / -oil 65
recommend / -end 41
record / -oard 62
recount / -ount 82
recoup / -oop 74
rectangle / -angle 20
red / -ed 35
redeem / -eam 30
redhead / -ed 35
reduce / -oose 74
reed / -eed 36
reef / -eaf 30
reek / -eek 37
reel / -eal 30
referee / -e 29
refereed / -eed 36
referees / -ees 38
refill / -ill 52
reflect / -ect 34
refresh / -esh 42
refrigerate / -ate 25
refuel / -ool 72
refugee / -e 29
refugees / -ees 38
refuse / -use 96
regret / -et 44
regroup / -oop 74
reign / -ane 20
reimburse / -urse 95
rein / -ane 20
reindeer / -ear 31
reinforce / -orse 79
reject / -ect 34
rejoin / -oin 65
relax / -acks 11
release / -eece 36
released / -east 32
relent / -ent 41
relied / -ide 48
relief / -eaf 30
relieve / -eve 44
rely / -i 45
remain / -ane 20
remark / -ark 22
remind / -ind 55
remorse / -orse 79
remote / -oat 63
rendezvous / -oo 70
renew / -oo 70
renewed / -ude 88
renowned / -ound 82
rent / -ent 41
repaid / -ade 12
repair / -air 15
repeat / -eat 32
rephrase / aze 28
replace / -ace 9
replaced / -aced 9
replayed / ade 12
replied / -ide 48
replies / -ies 49
reply / -i 45
report / -ort 79
represent / -ent 41
repress / -ess 42
reprieve / -eve 44
reprint / -int 57
reptile / -ile 52
request / -est 43
reread / -eed 36
rescue / -oo 71
rescued / -ude 88
resent / -ent 41
residue / -oo 71
resign / -ine 55
resist / -ist 58
resort / -ort 79
respect / -ect 34
respond / -ond 69
rest / -est 43
restful / -ul 90
restored / -oard 62
restores / -ores 77
retell / -ell 39
rethink / -ink 56
retold / -old 66
retrace / -ace 9
retraced / -aced 9
retreat / -eat 32
retrieve / -eve 44
return / -urn 94
reveal / -eal 30
reverberate / -ate 25
revere / -ear 31
reverse / -urse 95
review / -oo 70
revive / -ive 60
revolt / -olt 67
revue / -oo 71
reward / -oard 62
rewind / -ind 55
rewrote / -oat 63
rhino / -o 61
rhinos / -ows 85
rhyme / -ime 54
rib / -ib 46
rice / -ice 46
rich / -itch 60
ricochet / -ay 27
rid / -id 47
riddle / -iddle 47
ride / -ide 48
ridge / -idge 49
ridicule / -ool 72
rift / -ift 50
right / -ight 51
rigid / -id 47
rigmarole / -ole 67
rim / -im 53
rind / -ind 55
ring / -ing 56
rink / -ink 56
RIP / -e 29

rip / **-ip** 57
ripe / **-ipe** 57
rise / **-ies** 49
risk / **-isk** 58
river / **-iver** 60
riverside / **-ide** 48
road / **-oad** 62
roadblock / **-ock** 64
roadside / **-ide** 48
roam / **-ome** 68
roar / **-ore** 76
roared / **-oard** 62
roaring / **-ing** 56
roars / **-ores** 77
roast / **-ost** 80
rob / **-ob** 63
robe / **-obe** 64
robin / **-in** 54
robot / **-ot** 81
rock / **-ock** 64
rockabye / **-i** 45
rocket / **-it** 59
rocks / **-ocks** 64
rocky / **-ocky** 64
rod / **-od** 65
rode / **-oad** 62
rodeos / **-ows** 85
role / **-ole** 67
roll / **-ole** 67
rolled / **-old** 66
romantic / **-antic** 21
Rome / **-ome** 68
rooftop / **-op** 75
rook / **-ook** 72
room / **-oom** 73
roomful / **-ul** 90
root / **-ute** 98
rope / **-ope** 75
rose / **-ows** 85
rosebud / **-ud** 88
rosette / **-et** 44
rot / **-ot** 81
rotate / **-ate** 25
rote / **-oat** 63
rough / **-uff** 89
roulette / **-et** 44
round / **-ound** 82
roundabout / **-out** 83
Roundhead / **-ed** 35
routine / **-een** 37
row / **-o** 61
row / **-ow** 83
rowboat / **-oat** 63
rowed / **-oad** 62
rowed / **-oud** 82
rows / **-ows** 85
royal / **-oil** 65
RSVP / **-e** 29
rub / **-ub** 87
rub-a-dub-dub / **-ub** 87
rubbish / **-ish** 58
rubble / **-ubble** 87
rucksack / **-ack** 10
rucksacks / **-acks** 11
rude / **-ude** 88
rue / **-oo** 71
rug / **-ug** 89
ruin / **-in** 54
rule / **-ool** 72
rum / **-um** 90
rumble / **-umble** 91
rump / **-ump** 91
rumpsteak / **-ake** 16
rumpus / **-us** 96
run / **-un** 92
runaway / **-ay** 27
runaways / **-aze** 28
rung / **-ung** 92
running / **-ing** 56
runt / **-unt** 93
runway / **-ay** 27
runways / **-aze** 28
rupee / **-e** 29
rupees / **-ees** 38
ruse / **-use** 96
rush / **-ush** 97
rusk / **-usk** 97
rust / **-ust** 97
rut / **-ut** 97
rye / **-i** 45

S

sable / **-able** 8
sac / **-ack** 10
sachet / **-ay** 27
sack / **-ack** 10
sacked / **-act** 11
sackful / **-ul** 90
sacks / **-acks** 11
sacrifice / **-ice** 46
sad / **-ad** 12
saddlebag / **-ag** 13
sag / **-ag** 13
said / **-ed** 35
sail / **-ale** 14
sailboat / **-oat** 63
sake / **-ake** 16
sale / **-ale** 14
salon / **-on** 68
salute / **-ute** 98
same / **-ame** 18
sand / **-and** 19
sandbag / **-ag** 13
sandbank / **-ank** 21
sandman / **-an** 18
sandstorm / **-orm** 78
sandwich / **-itch** 60
sane / **-ane** 20
sang / **-ang** 20
sank / **-ank** 21
sap / **-ap** 21
sapphire / **-ire** 57
sardine / **-een** 37
sarong / **-ong** 69
sash / **-ash** 23
sat / **-at** 24
satellite / **-ight** 51
satin / **-in** 54
satisfied / **-ide** 48
satisfy / **-i** 45
Saturday / **-ay** 27
sauce / **-orse** 79
save / **-ave** 27
saw / **-ore** 76
sawdust / **-ust** 97
sawmill / **-ill** 52
sawn / **-orn** 78
saws / **-ores** 77
sax / **-acks** 11
saxophone / **-one** 69
say / **-ay** 27
scab / **-ab** 8
scaffold / **-old** 66
scale / **-ale** 14
scallywag / **-ag** 13
scam / **-am** 17
scamp / **-amp** 18
scamper / **-amper** 18
scan / **-an** 18
scanned / **-and** 19
scant / **-ant** 21
scapegoat / **-oat** 63
scar / **-a** 8
scare / **-air** 15
scarecrow / **-o** 61
scarecrows / **-ows** 85
scarf / **-arf** 22
scarred / **-ard** 22
scary / **-airy** 16
scatter / **-atter** 26
scatterbrain / **-ane** 20
scatty / **-atty** 26
schedule / **-ool** 72
scene / **-een** 37
scent / **-ent** 41
scheme / **-eam** 30
school / **-ool** 72
schoolboy / **-oy** 86
schoolboys / **-oise** 66
schoolbus / **-us** 96
schoolmate / **-ate** 25
sci-fi / **-i** 45
scold / **-old** 66
scone / **-on** 68
scone / **-one** 69
scoop / **-oop** 74
scoot / **-ute** 98
scope / **-ope** 75
score / **-ore** 76
scoreboard / **-oard** 62
scorecard / **-ard** 22
scored / **-oard** 62
scores / **-ores** 77
scorn / **-orn** 78
Scot / **-ot** 81
scour / **-ower** 84
scout / **-out** 83
scowl / **-owl** 84
scrabble / **-abble** 8
scram / **-am** 17
scrap / **-ap** 21
scrapbook / **-ook** 72
scrape / **-ape** 21
scrapyard / **-ard** 22
scratch / **-atch** 24
scrawl / **-all** 17
scream / **-eam** 30
screen / **-een** 37
screw / **-oo** 70
screwed / **-ude** 88
scribble / **-ibble** 46
scroll / **-ole** 67
scrub / **-ub** 87
scruff / **-uff** 89
scrum / **-um** 90
scrunch / **-unch** 92
scud / **-ud** 88
scuff / **-uff** 89
scum / **-um** 90

scut / **-ut** 97
sea / **-e** 29
seaborne / **-orn** 78
seadog / **-og** 65
seafood / **-ude** 88
seahorse / **-orse** 79
seal / **-eal** 30
seam / **-eam** 30
seaport / **-ort** 79
searchlight / **-ight** 51
seas / **-ees** 38
seascape / **-ape** 21
seashell / **-ell** 39
seashore / **-ore** 76
seasick / **-ick** 46
seaside / **-ide** 48
seat / **-eat** 32
seatbelt / **-elt** 40
seaweed / **-eed** 36
secondhand / **-and** 19
secret / **-it** 59
sect / **-ect** 34
see / **-e** 29
seed / **-eed** 36
seek / **-eek** 37
seem / **-eam** 30
seen / **-een** 37
seep / **-eep** 38
sees / **-ees** 38
seesaw / **-ore** 76
seesaws / **-ores** 77
seize / **-ees** 38
select / **-ect** 34
self-defence / **-ence** 40
self-esteem / **-eam** 30
selfish / **-ish** 58
self-service / **-iss** 58
sell / **-ell** 39
send / **-end** 41
sender / **-ender** 41
sense / **-ence** 40
sent / **-ent** 41
separate / **-ate** 25
sequin / **-in** 54
serene / **-een** 37
serious / **-us** 96
service / **-iss** 58
serviette / **-et** 44
set / **-et** 44
setback / **-ack** 10
setbacks / **-acks** 11
settee / **-e** 29
settle / **-ettle** 44
seventeen / **-een** 37
severe / **-ear** 31
sew / **-o** 61
sewn / **-one** 69
shabby / **-abby** 8
shack / **-ack** 10
shackle / **-ackle** 10
shacks / **-acks** 11
shade / **-ade** 12
shadow / **-o** 61
shadowed / **-oad** 62
shadows / **-ows** 85
shaft / **-aft** 13
shake / **-ake** 16
shallow / **-o** 61
sham / **-am** 17
shame / **-ame** 18
shamefaced / **-aced** 9
shameful / **-ul** 90
shampoo / **-oo** 70
shampooed / **-ude** 88
shamrock / **-ock** 64
shantytown / **-own** 84
shape / **-ape** 21
shard / **-ard** 22
share / **-air** 15
shark / **-ark** 22
shatter / **-atter** 26
shave / **-ave** 27
shawl / **-all** 17
she / **-e** 29
sheaf / **-eaf** 30
shear / **-ear** 31
shed / **-ed** 35
sheen / **-een** 37
sheep / **-eep** 38
sheepish / **-ish** 58
sheepskin / **-in** 54
sheer / **-ear** 31
sheet / **-eat** 32
shell / **-ell** 39
shellfish / **-ish** 58
shift / **-ift** 50
shin / **-in** 54
shinbone / **-one** 69
shine / **-ine** 55
ship / **-ip** 57
shipmate / **-ate** 25
shipshape / **-ape** 21
shipwreck / **-eck** 33
shipwrecked / **-ect** 34
shipwrecks / **-ecks** 34
shirk / **-urk** 94
shirt / **-urt** 96
shiver / **-iver** 60
shoal / **-ole** 67
shock / **-ock** 64
shocks / **-ocks** 64
shockwave / **-ave** 27
shod / **-od** 65
shoe / **-oo** 70
shoelace / **-ace** 9
shoeshine / **-ine** 55
shone / **-on** 68
shoo / **-oo** 70
shooed / **-ude** 88
shook / **-ook** 72
shoot / **-ute** 98
shootout / **-out** 83
shop / **-op** 75
shoplift / **-ift** 50
shore / **-ore** 76
shores / **-ores** 77
shorn / **-orn** 78
short / **-ort** 79
shortbread / **-ed** 35
shortcut / **-ut** 97
shot / **-ot** 81
shotgun / **-un** 92
should / **-ood** 72
shout / **-out** 83
show / **-o** 61
showbiz / **-is** 58
showdown / **-own** 84
showed / **-oad** 62
shower / **-ower** 84
shown / **-one** 69
shows / **-ows** 85
shrank / **-ank** 21
shred / **-ed** 35
shrew / **-oo** 70
shriek / **-eek** 37
shrill / **-ill** 52
shrink / **-ink** 56
shroud / **-oud** 82
shrub / **-ub** 87
shrug / **-ug** 89
shrunk / **-unk** 93
shun / **-un** 92
shunt / **-unt** 93
shush / **-ush** 97
shut / **-ut** 97
shutter / **-utter** 98
shuttlecock / **-ock** 64
shy / **-i** 45
Sicily / **-illy** 53
sick / **-ick** 46
sickbed / **-ed** 35
side / **-ide** 48
sideshow / **-o** 61
sideshows / **-ows** 85
sidestepped / **-ept** 42
sidetrack / **-ack** 10
sidetracked / **-act** 11
sidetracks / **-acks** 11
sideways / **-aze** 28
sift / **-ift** 50
sigh / **-i** 45
sighed / **-ide** 48
sighs / **-ies** 49
sight / **-ight** 51
sightsee / **-e** 29
sightsees / **-ees** 38
sign / **-ine** 55
signed / **-ind** 55
signpost / **-ost** 80
silhouette / **-et** 44
sill / **-ill** 52
silly / **-illy** 53
silly-billy / **-illy** 53
simplify / **-i** 45
simulator / **-ator** 26
sin / **-in** 54
Sinbad / **-ad** 12
sincere / **-ear** 31
sinew / **-oo** 70
sing / **-ing** 56
singe / **-inge** 56
sink / **-ink** 56
sip / **-ip** 57
sir / **-ur** 94
sirloin / **-oin** 65
sisterhood / **-ood** 72
sit / **-it** 59
sitar / **-a** 8
site / **-ight** 51
sitter / **-itter** 60
sitting / **-ing** 56
six / **-icks** 47
sixteen / **-een** 37
size / **-ies** 49
skate / **-ate** 25
skateboard / **-oard** 62
skater / **-ator** 26
skating / **-ing** 56
sketch / **-etch** 44
sketchbook / **-ook** 72
skew / **-oo** 70

skewwhiff / **-iff** 49
ski / **-e** 29
skid / **-id** 47
skidoo / **-oo** 70
skies / **-ies** 49
skilful / **-ul** 90
skill / **-ill** 52
skim / **-im** 53
skin / **-in** 54
skinflint / **-int** 57
skinhead / **-ed** 35
skint / **-int** 57
skintight / **-ight** 51
skip / **-ip** 57
skirt / **-urt** 96
skitter / **-itter** 60
skunk / **-unk** 93
sky / **-i** 45
skydive / **-ive** 60
skylark / **-ark** 22
skylight / **-ight** 51
skyline / **-ine** 55
slab / **-ab** 8
slack / **-ack** 10
slacked / **-act** 11
slam / **-am** 17
slang / **-ang** 20
slants / **-ance** 19
slap / **-ap** 21
slapdash / **-ash** 23
slash / **-ash** 23
slave / **-ave** 27
sled / **-ed** 35
sledge / **-edge** 35
sleek / **-eek** 37
sleep / **-eep** 38
sleepwalk / **-ork** 78
sleepyhead / **-ed** 35
sleet / **-eat** 32
sleeve / **-eve** 44
sleigh / **-ay** 27
sleighed / **-ade** 12
slender / **-ender** 41
slept / **-ept** 42
slew / **-oo** 70
slice / **-ice** 46
slick / **-ick** 46
slid / **-id** 47
slide / **-ide** 48
slight / **-ight** 51
slim / **-im** 53
slime / **-ime** 54
sling / **-ing** 56
slink / **-ink** 56
slip / **-ip** 57
slipstream / **-eam** 30
slit / **-it** 59
sliver / **-iver** 60
slob / **-ob** 63
slog / **-og** 65
sloop / **-oop** 74
slop / **-op** 75
slope / **-ope** 75
slosh / **-osh** 80
slot / **-ot** 81
slouch / **-ouch** 81
slow / **-o** 61
slowdown / **-own** 84
slowed / **-oad** 62
slows / **-ows** 85
sludge / **-udge** 89
slug / **-ug** 89
sluice / **-oose** 74
slum / **-um** 90
slump / **-ump** 91
slung / **-ung** 92
slunk / **-unk** 93
slur / **-ur** 94
slurred / **-urred** 95
slush / **-ush** 97
sly / **-i** 45
smack / **-ack** 10
smacked / **-act** 11
smacks / **-acks** 11
small / **-all** 17
smart / **-art** 23
smash / **-ash** 23
smear / **-ear** 31
smell / **-ell** 39
smile / **-ile** 52
smiled / **-ild** 52
smirk / **-urk** 94
smog / **-og** 65
smoke / **-oke** 66
smokescreen / **-een** 37
smudge / **-udge** 89
smug / **-ug** 89
smut / **-ut** 97
snack / **-ack** 10
snacked / **-act** 11
snacks / **-acks** 11
snag / **-ag** 13
snail / **-ale** 14
snake / **-ake** 16
snakelike / **-ike** 51
snap / **-ap** 21
snapshot / **-ot** 81
snare / **-air** 15
snatch / **-atch** 24
sneak / **-eek** 37
sneer / **-ear** 31
sneeze / **-ees** 38
sneezy / **-easy** 32
sniff / **-iff** 49
sniffed / **-ift** 50
snip / **-ip** 57
snitch / **-itch** 60
snob / **-ob** 63
snoop / **-oop** 74
snore / **-ore** 76
snored / **-oard** 62
snores / **-ores** 77
snort / **-ort** 79
snot / **-ot** 81
snout / **-out** 83
snow / **-o** 61
snowball / **-all** 17
snowboard / **-oard** 62
snowdrift / **-ift** 50
snowdrop / **-op** 75
snowed / **-oad** 62
snowfall / **-all** 17
snowflake / **-ake** 16
snowmobile / **-eal** 30
snowplough / **-ow** 83
snows / **-ows** 85
snowshoe / **-oo** 70
snowstorm / **-orm** 78
snub / **-ub** 87
snuff / **-uff** 89
snug / **-ug** 89
so / **-o** 61
soak / **-oke** 66
so-and-sos / **-ows** 85
soap / **-ope** 75
soar / **-ore** 76
soared / **-oard** 62
soars / **-ores** 77
sob / **-ob** 63
sock / **-ock** 64
socks / **-ocks** 64
software / **-air** 15
soil / **-oil** 65
sold / **-old** 66
sole / **-ole** 67
soled / **-old** 66
solitaire / **-air** 15
solitude / **-ude** 88
solo / **-o** 61
some / **-um** 90
somehow / **-ow** 83
someone / **-un** 92
something / **-ing** 56
sometime / **-ime** 54
somewhat / **-ot** 81
somewhere / **-air** 15
son / **-un** 92
song / **-ong** 69
songbird / **-urred** 95
songbook / **-ook** 72
songthrush / **-ush** 97
soon / **-oon** 73
soot / **-oot** 74
sore / **-ore** 76
sores / **-ores** 77
sorrow / **-o** 61
sorrowful / **-ul** 90
sort / **-ort** 79
soul / **-ole** 67
sound / **-ound** 82
soundtrack / **-ack** 10
soundtracks / **-acks** 11
soup / **-oop** 74
sour / **-ower** 84
southbound / **-ound** 82
southeast / **-east** 32
southwest / **-est** 43
souvenir / **-ear** 31
sow / **-o** 61
sow / **-ow** 83
sown / **-one** 69
sows / **-ows** 85
space / **-ace** 9
spacecraft / **-aft** 13
spaced / **-aced** 9
spaceship / **-ip** 57
spacesuit / **-ute** 98
spacewalk / **-ork** 78
spade / **-ade** 12
Spain / **-ane** 20
span / **-an** 18
spangle / **-angle** 20
spank / **-ank** 21
spanned / **-and** 19
spar / **-a** 8
spare / **-air** 15
spark / **-ark** 22
sparred / **-ard** 22
spat / **-at** 24
speak / **-eek** 37
spear / **-ear** 31
spearmint / **-int** 57

specify / **-i** 45
speck / **-eck** 33
specks / **-ecks** 34
spectator / **-ator** 26
spectrum / **-um** 90
sped / **-ed** 35
speed / **-eed** 36
speedboat / **-oat** 63
spell / **-ell** 39
spellbound / **-ound** 82
spelling / **-ing** 56
spend / **-end** 41
spendthrift / **-ift** 50
spent / **-ent** 41
sphere / **-ear** 31
spice / **-ice** 46
spied / **-ide** 48
spies / **-ies** 49
spike / **-ike** 51
spill / **-ill** 52
spilt / **-ilt** 53
spin / **-in** 54
spine / **-ine** 55
spine-chilling / **-ing** 56
spire / **-ire** 57
spit / **-it** 59
spite / **-ight** 51
splash / **-ash** 23
splashdown / **-own** 84
splat / **-at** 24
splatter / **-atter** 26
spleen / **-een** 37
splice / **-ice** 46
splint / **-int** 57
split / **-it** 59
splutter / **-utter** 98
spoil / **-oil** 65
spoilsport / **-ort** 79
spoke / **-oke** 66
spool / **-ool** 72
spoon / **-oon** 73
spoonfed / **-ed** 35
spoonful / **-ul** 90
sport / **-ort** 79
sportswear / **-air** 15
spot / **-ot** 81
spotlight / **-ight** 51
spotty / **-otty** 81
spout / **-out** 83
sprain / **-ane** 20
sprang / **-ang** 20
sprawl / **-all** 17
spray / **-ay** 27
sprayed / **-ade** 12
sprays / **-aze** 28
spread / **-ed** 35
spree / **-e** 29
sprees / **-ees** 38
sprig / **-ig** 50
spring / **-ing** 56
springboard / **-oard** 62
springtime / **-ime** 54
sprite / **-ight** 51
sprout / **-out** 83
spruce / **-oose** 74
sprung / **-ung** 92
spud / **-ud** 88
spun / **-un** 92
spur / **-ur** 94
spurn / **-urn** 94
spurred / **-urred** 95
spurt / **-urt** 96
spy / **-i** 45
spyglass / **-ass** 24
squabble / **-obble** 63
squall / **-all** 17
square / **-air** 15
squash / **-osh** 80
squat / **-ot** 81
squaw / **-ore** 76
squawk / **-ork** 78
squeak / **-eek** 37
squeal / **-eal** 30
squeeze / **-ees** 38
squid / **-id** 47
squidge / **-idge** 49
squiggle / **-iggle** 50
squint / **-int** 57
squirt / **-urt** 96
squish / **-ish** 58
stab / **-ab** 8
stable / **-able** 8
stack / **-ack** 10
stacked / **-act** 11
stacks / **-acks** 11
stadium / **-um** 90
stag / **-ag** 13
stage / **-age** 13
stagestruck / **-uck** 87
staid / **-ade** 12
stain / **-ane** 20
stair / **-air** 15
staircase / **-ace** 9
stake / **-ake** 16
stalactite / **-ight** 51
stalagmite / **-ight** 51
stale / **-ale** 14
stalemate / **-ate** 25
stalk / **-ork** 78
stall / **-all** 17
stamp / **-amp** 18
stampede / **-eed** 36
stance / **-ance** 19
stand / **-and** 19
stand-in / **-in** 54
standstill / **-ill** 52
stank / **-ank** 21
star / **-a** 8
starch / **-arch** 22
stardom / **-um** 90
stardust / **-ust** 97
stare / **-air** 15
starfish / **-ish** 58
starfruit / **-ute** 98
stargaze / **-aze** 28
starlight / **-ight** 51
starred / **-ard** 22
start / **-art** 23
stash / **-ash** 23
state / **-ate** 25
state-of-the-art / **-art** 23
statue / **-oo** 71
stay / **-ay** 27
stayed / **-ade** 12
stays / **-aze** 28
stead / **-ed** 35
steadily / **-illy** 53
steak / **-ake** 16
steal / **-eal** 30
steam / **-eam** 30
steamroll / **-ole** 67
steamrolled / **-old** 66
steed / **-eed** 36
steel / **-eal** 30
steep / **-eep** 38
steer / **-ear** 31
stem / **-em** 40
stench / **-ench** 40
stepped / **-ept** 42
stepson / **-un** 92
stereo / **-o** 61
stereos / **-ows** 85
stereotype / **-ipe** 57
stern / **-urn** 94
stethoscope / **-ope** 75
stetson / **-un** 92
stew / **-oo** 70
stewed / **-ude** 88
stews / **-use** 96
stick / **-ick** 46
stickleback / **-ack** 10
sticks / **-icks** 47
stiff / **-iff** 49
stile / **-ile** 52
still / **-ill** 52
stilt / **-ilt** 53
sting / **-ing** 56
stink / **-ink** 56
stir / **-ur** 94
stitch / **-itch** 60
stoat / **-oat** 63
stock / **-ock** 64
stocky / **-ocky** 64
stole / **-ole** 67
stone / **-one** 69
stood / **-ood** 72
stool / **-ool** 72
stoop / **-oop** 74
stop / **-op** 75
store / **-ore** 76
stored / **-oard** 62
storeroom / **-oom** 73
stores / **-ores** 77
stork / **-ork** 78
storm / **-orm** 78
storybook / **-ook** 72
storyline / **-ine** 55
stow / **-o** 61
stowaway / **-ay** 27
stowaways / **-aze** 28
stowed / **-oad** 62
stows / **-ows** 85
straight / **-ate** 25
straightaway / **-ay** 27
strain / **-ane** 20
straitlaced / **-aced** 9
strand / **-and** 19
strangle / **-angle** 20
strap / **-ap** 21
stratosphere / **-ear** 31
straw / **-ore** 76
strawberry / **-erry** 42
straws / **-ores** 77
stray / **-ay** 27
strayed / **-ade** 12
strays / **-aze** 28
stream / **-eam** 30
streamlined / **-ind** 55
street / **-eat** 32
streetlight / **-ight** 51
stress / **-ess** 42
stressed / **-est** 43

stretch / **-etch** 44
stride / **-ide** 48
strike / **-ike** 51
string / **-ing** 56
strip / **-ip** 57
stripe / **-ipe** 57
strobe / **-obe** 64
strode / **-oad** 62
stroke / **-oke** 66
stroll / **-ole** 67
strolled / **-old** 66
strong / **-ong** 69
stronghold / **-old** 66
strongroom / **-oom** 73
struck / **-uck** 87
strum / **-um** 90
strung / **-ung** 92
strut / **-ut** 97
stub / **-ub** 87
stubble / **-ubble** 87
stuck / **-uck** 87
stud / **-ud** 88
studio / **-o** 61
studios / **-ows** 85
stuff / **-uff** 89
stumble / **-umble** 91
stump / **-ump** 91
stun / **-un** 92
stung / **-ung** 92
stunning / **-ing** 56
stunt / **-unt** 93
stupendous / **-us** 96
stupify / **-i** 45
stutter / **-utter** 98
sty / **-i** 45
style / **-ile** 52
subdue / **-oo** 71
subject / **-ect** 34
submarine / **-een** 37
substitute / **-ute** 98
subtract / **-act** 11
subway / **-ay** 27
subways / **-aze** 28
succeed / **-eed** 36
success / **-ess** 42
succumb / **-um** 90
such / **-uch** 87
suck / **-uck** 87
suckle / **-uckle** 88
sue / **-oo** 71
sued / **-ude** 88
suede / **-ade** 12
sugarbowl / **-ole** 67
suggest / **-est** 43
suit / **-ute** 98
suitcase / **-ace** 9
sum / **-um** 90
summertime / **-ime** 54
summit / **-it** 59
sun / **-un** 92
sunbeam / **-eam** 30
sunblock / **-ock** 64
sunburn / **-urn** 94
suncream / **-eam** 30
Sunday / **-ay** 27
Sundays / **-aze** 28
sundial / **-ile** 52
sundown / **-own** 84
sundress / **-ess** 42
sunflower / **-ower** 84
sung / **-ung** 92
sunhat / **-at** 24
sunk / **-unk** 93
sunlight / **-ight** 51
sunlit / **-it** 59
sunrise / **-ies** 49
sunscreen / **-een** 37
sunset / **-et** 44
sunshade / **-ade** 12
sunshine / **-ine** 55
sunspot / **-ot** 81
sunstroke / **-oke** 66
suntan / **-an** 18
suntrap / **-ap** 21
supercool / **-ool** 72
supersonic / **-ick** 46
superstar / **-a** 8
suppertime / **-ime** 54
support / **-ort** 79
suppose / **-ows** 85
supreme / **-eam** 30
surfboard / **-oard** 62
surname / **-ame** 18
surpass / **-ass** 24
surpassed / **-ast** 24
surprise / **-ies** 49
surprising / **-ing** 56
surrender / **-ender** 41
surround / **-ound** 82
survey / **-ay** 27
surveyed / **-ade** 12
survive / **-ive** 60
suspect / **-ect** 34
suspend / **-end** 41
suspense / **-ence** 40
suss / **-us** 96
swag / **-ag** 13
swam / **-am** 17
swan / **-on** 68
swank / **-ank** 21
swarm / **-orm** 78
swashbuckle / **-uckle** 88
swat / **-ot** 81
sway / **-ay** 27
swayed / **-ade** 12
sways / **-aze** 28
swear / **-air** 15
swearword / **-urred** 95
sweat / **-et** 44
sweatband / **-and** 19
sweatshirt / **-urt** 96
swede / **-eed** 36
sweep / **-eep** 38
sweet / **-eat** 32
sweetcorn / **-orn** 78
sweeter / **-eater** 33
sweetheart / **-art** 23
sweetshop / **-op** 75
swell / **-ell** 39
swept / **-ept** 42
swift / **-ift** 50
swig / **-ig** 50
swill / **-ill** 52
swim / **-im** 53
swimsuit / **-ute** 98
swine / **-ine** 55
swing / **-ing** 56
swingboat / **-oat** 63
swipe / **-ipe** 57
swirl / **-url** 94
swish / **-ish** 58
switch / **-itch** 60
switchback / **-ack** 10
switchbacks / **-acks** 11
swizz / **-is** 58
swoon / **-oon** 73
swoop / **-oop** 74
sword / **-oard** 62
swore / **-ore** 76
sworn / **-orn** 78
swot / **-ot** 81
swum / **-um** 90
swung / **-ung** 92
sycamore / **-ore** 76
sycamores / **-ores** 77
synagogue / **-og** 65
synonym / **-im** 53
syringe / **-inge** 56

t

tabby / **-abby** 8
table / **-able** 8
tablespoon / **-oon** 73
tackle / **-ackle** 10
tact / **-act** 11
tactic / **-ick** 46
tadpole / **-ole** 67
tag / **-ag** 13
tail / **-ale** 14
tailback / **-ack** 10
tailspin / **-in** 54
take / **-ake** 16
takeaway / **-ay** 27
tale / **-ale** 14
talk / **-ork** 78
tall / **-all** 17
tally / **-alley** 17
tambourine / **-een** 37
tame / **-ame** 18
tamper / **-amper** 18
tan / **-an** 18
tang / **-ang** 20
tangerine / **-een** 37
tangle / **-angle** 20
tank / **-ank** 21
tanned / **-and** 19
tantrum / **-um** 90
tap / **-ap** 21
tape / **-ape** 21
tar / **-a** 8
tarmac / **-ack** 10
tarred / **-ard** 22
tart / **-art** 23
task / **-ask** 23
taste / **-aced** 9
tastebud / **-ud** 88
tattoo / **-oo** 70
tattooed / **-ude** 88
tattoos / **-use** 96
tatty / **-atty** 26
taught / **-ort** 79
taut / **-ort** 79
tax / **-acks** 11
tea / **-e** 29
teabag / **-ag** 13
teacake / **-ake** 16
teacup / **-up** 93
team / **-eam** 30

teamwork / **-urk** 94
teapot / **-ot** 81
tear / **-air** 15
tear / **-ear** 31
teardrop / **-op** 75
tearful / **-ul** 90
tearoom / **-oom** 73
tearstain / **-ane** 20
tease / **-ees** 38
teashop / **-op** 75
teaspoon / **-oon** 73
teat / **-eat** 32
teatime / **-ime** 54
technique / **-eek** 37
tee / **-e** 29
tee-hee / **-e** 29
teem / **-eam** 30
teen / **-een** 37
teenage / **-age** 13
teepee / **-e** 29
teepees / **-ees** 38
teeter / **-eater** 33
telephone / **-one** 69
telescope / **-ope** 75
televise / **-ies** 49
tell / **-ell** 39
telltale / **-ale** 14
ten / **-en** 40
tend / **-end** 41
tender / **-ender** 41
tennis / **-iss** 58
tense / **-ence** 40
tent / **-ent** 41
terrapin / **-in** 54
terrific / **-ick** 46
terrified / **-ide** 48
terrifies / **-ies** 49
terrify / **-i** 45
test / **-est** 43
textbook / **-ook** 72
than / **-an** 18
thank / **-ank** 21
that / **-at** 24
thatch / **-atch** 24
thaw / **-ore** 76
thaws / **-ores** 77
their / **-air** 15
them / **-em** 40
theme / **-eam** 30
then / **-en** 40
there / **-air** 15
therefore / **-ore** 76
thesaurus / **-us** 96
these / **-ees** 38
they / **-ay** 27
thick / **-ick** 46
thief / **-eaf** 30
thigh / **-i** 45
thighbone / **-one** 69
thighs / **-ies** 49
thin / **-in** 54
thing / **-ing** 56
thingamabob / **-ob** 63
think / **-ink** 56
third / **-urred** 95
thirteen / **-een** 37
this / **-iss** 58
thorax / **-acks** 11
thorn / **-orn** 78
those / **-ows** 85
though / **-o** 61
thought / **-ort** 79
thrash / **-ash** 23
thread / **-ed** 35
threadbare / **-air** 15
threat / **-et** 44
three / **-e** 29
threesome / **-um** 90
thresh / **-esh** 42
threw / **-oo** 70
thrift / **-ift** 50
thrill / **-ill** 52
throat / **-oat** 63
throb / **-ob** 63
throes / **-ows** 85
throne / **-one** 69
throng / **-ong** 69
through / **-oo** 70
throughout / **-out** 83
throw / **-o** 61
thrown / **-one** 69
throws / **-ows** 85
thrush / **-ush** 97
thrust / **-ust** 97
thud / **-ud** 88
thug / **-ug** 89
thumb / **-um** 90
thumbnail / **-ale** 14
thumbprint / **-int** 57
thump / **-ump** 91
thunder / **-under** 92
thunderbolt / **-olt** 67
thunderclap / **-ap** 21
thundercloud / **-oud** 82
thunderstorm / **-orm** 78
thunderstruck / **-uck** 87
Thursday / **-ay** 27
thus / **-us** 96
thwack / **-ack** 10
thwacked / **-act** 11
thwacks / **-acks** 11
thwart / **-ort** 79
thyme / **-ime** 54
Tibet / **-et** 44
tick / **-ick** 46
ticket / **-it** 59
ticks / **-icks** 47
tick-tock / **-ock** 64
tick-tocks / **-ocks** 64
tics / **-icks** 47
tide / **-ide** 48
tie / **-i** 45
tied / **-ide** 48
tier / **-ear** 31
ties / **-ies** 49
tiff / **-iff** 49
tigerskin / **-in** 54
tight / **-ight** 51
tightrope / **-ope** 75
tile / **-ile** 52
tiled / **-ild** 52
till / **-ill** 52
tilt / **-ilt** 53
time / **-ime** 54
timepiece / **-eece** 36
timetable / **-able** 8
timid / **-id** 47
tin / **-in** 54
tinfoil / **-oil** 65
tinge / **-inge** 56
tint / **-int** 57
tip / **-ip** 57
tiptoe / **-o** 61
tiptoes / **-ows** 85
tire / **-ire** 57
tissue / **-oo** 71
tittle-tattle / **-attle** 26
to / **-oo** 70
toad / **-oad** 62
toadstool / **-ool** 72
toast / **-ost** 80
today / **-ay** 27
toe / **-o** 61
toenail / **-ale** 14
toes / **-ows** 85
toffee / **-e** 29
toffees / **-ees** 38
toil / **-oil** 65
told / **-old** 66
tomahawk / **-ork** 78
tomboy / **-oy** 86
tombstone / **-one** 69
tomcat / **-at** 24
tomorrow / **-o** 61
ton / **-un** 92
tone / **-one** 69
tongue / **-ung** 92
tonight / **-ight** 51
too / **-oo** 70
took / **-ook** 72
tool / **-ool** 72
toolshed / **-ed** 35
toot / **-ute** 98
toothache / **-ake** 16
toothbrush / **-ush** 97
toothpaste / **-aced** 9
top / **-op** 75
topknot / **-ot** 81
topsoil / **-oil** 65
tore / **-ore** 76
torment / **-ent** 41
torn / **-orn** 78
tornado / **-o** 61
toss / **-oss** 80
tot / **-ot** 81
touch / **-uch** 87
touchdown / **-own** 84
touchline / **-ine** 55
tough / **-uff** 89
tourist / **-ist** 58
tow / **-o** 61
toward / **-oard** 62
towbar / **-a** 8
towed / **-oad** 62
towel / **-owl** 84
tower / **-ower** 84
town / **-own** 84
townsfolk / **-oke** 66
towrope / **-ope** 75
tows / **-ows** 85
toy / **-oy** 86
toys / **-oise** 66
trace / **-ace** 9
traced / **-aced** 9
track / **-ack** 10
tracked / **-act** 11
tracks / **-acks** 11
tracksuit / **-ute** 98
trade / **-ade** 12
tragic / **-ick** 46
trail / **-ale** 14

trailblaze / **-aze** 28
train / **-ane** 20
traitor / **-ator** 26
tra-la-la / **-a** 8
tram / **-am** 17
tramp / **-amp** 18
trampoline / **-een** 37
trance / **-ance** 19
tranquil / **-ill** 52
transatlantic / **-antic** 21
transfer / **-ur** 94
translate / **-ate** 25
translator / **-ator** 26
transmitter / **-itter** 60
transplants / **-ance** 19
transport / **-ort** 79
trap / **-ap** 21
trapdoor / **-ore** 76
trapdoors / **-ores** 77
trapeze / **-ees** 38
trash / **-ash** 23
trawl / **-all** 17
tray / **-ay** 27
trays / **-aze** 28
tread / **-ed** 35
treadmill / **-ill** 52
treat / **-eat** 32
tree / **-e** 29
trees / **-ees** 38
treetop / **-op** 75
trek / **-eck** 33
trellis / **-iss** 58
tremendous / **-us** 96
trench / **-ench** 40
trend / **-end** 41
tress / **-ess** 42
trial / **-ile** 52
triangle / **-angle** 20
tribute / **-ute** 98
trice / **-ice** 46
trick / **-ick** 46
tricks / **-icks** 47
tried / **-ide** 48
tries / **-ies** 49
trill / **-ill** 52
trim / **-im** 53
Trinidad / **-ad** 12
trip / **-ip** 57
triplet / **-it** 59
tripod / **-od** 65
trod / **-od** 65
trombone / **-one** 69
troop / **-oop** 74
tropics / **-icks** 47
trot / **-ot** 81
troubadour / **-ore** 76
troubadours / **-ores** 77
trouble / **-ubble** 87
troublesome / **-um** 90
troupe / **-oop** 74
trout / **-out** 83
trowel / **-owl** 84
truce / **-oose** 74
truck / **-uck** 87
truckload / **-oad** 62
trudge / **-udge** 89
true / **-oo** 71
trump / **-ump** 91
trumpet / **-it** 59
trunk / **-unk** 93
trust / **-ust** 97
try / **-i** 45
tsar / **-ar** 8
T-shirt / **-urt** 96
tub / **-ub** 87
tuck / **-uck** 87
Tuesday / **-ay** 27
tug / **-ug** 89
tulip / **-ip** 57
tum / **-um** 90
tumble / **-umble** 91
tummy / **-ummy** 91
tune / **-oon** 73
turboprop / **-op** 75
Turk / **-urk** 95
turmoil / **-oil** 65
turn / **-urn** 94
turnaround / **-ound** 82
turnstile / **-ile** 52
turntable / **-able** 8
turquoise / **-oise** 66
tusk / **-usk** 97
tut-tut / **-ut** 97
tutu / **-oo** 71
tu-whit tu-whoo / **-oo** 70
twang / **-ang** 20
tweak / **-eek** 37
tweed / **-eed** 36
tweet / **-eat** 32
twice / **-ice** 46
twiddle / **-iddle** 47
twig / **-ig** 50
twilight / **-ight** 51
twin / **-in** 54
twine / **-ine** 55
twinge / **-inge** 56
twirl / **-url** 94
twist / **-ist** 58
twit / **-it** 59
twitch / **-itch** 60
twitter / **-itter** 60
two / **-oo** 70
two-seater / **-eater** 33
twosome / **-um** 90
tycoon / **-oon** 73
type / **-ipe** 57
typhoon / **-oon** 73
tyre / **-ire** 57

u

UFO / **-o** 61
UFOs / **-ows** 85
umpteen / **-een** 37
unable / **-able** 8
unalike / **-ike** 51
unbend / **-end** 41
unbolt / **-olt** 67
unclear / **-ear** 31
uncoil / **-oil** 65
uncurl / **-url** 94
under / **-under** 92
underage / **-age** 13
underarm / **-arm** 23
undercut / **-ut** 97
underdog / **-og** 65
underfed / **-ed** 35
underfill / **-ill** 52
underfoot / **-oot** 74
underground / **-ound** 82
underhand / **-and** 19
underline / **-ine** 55
underlined / **-ind** 55
undermined / **-ind** 55
underpaid / **-ade** 12
underpass / **-ass** 24
underripe / **-ipe** 57
undersea / **-e** 29
understand / **-and** 19
understood / **-ood** 72
undertake / **-ake** 16
underwear / **-air** 15
underweight / **-ate** 25
undo / **-oo** 70
undone / **-un** 92
undress / **-ess** 42
undressed / **-est** 43
uneasy / **-easy** 32
unfair / **-air** 15
unfold / **-old** 66
unforeseen / **-een** 37
unfreeze / **-ees** 38
unfroze / **-ows** 85
unfurl / **-url** 94
unglue / **-oo** 71
unheard / **-urred** 95
unicorn / **-orn** 78
uniform / **-orm** 78
unimpressed / **-est** 43
unique / **-eek** 37
unite / **-ight** 51
universe / **-urse** 95
unjust / **-ust** 97
unkind / **-ind** 55
unknown / **-one** 69
unlace / **-ace** 9
unlaced / **-aced** 9
unlatch / **-atch** 24
unless / **-ess** 42
unlike / **-ike** 51
unload / **-oad** 62
unlock / **-ock** 64
unlocks / **-ocks** 64
unmade / **-ade** 12
unmask / **-ask** 23
unpack / **-ack** 10
unpacked / **-act** 11
unpacks / **-acks** 11
unpaid / **-ade** 12
unplug / **-ug** 89
unreal / **-eal** 30
unrest / **-est** 43
unripe / **-ipe** 57
unroll / **-ole** 67
unrolled / **-old** 66
unromantic / **-antic** 21
unscrew / **-oo** 70
unseen / **-een** 37
unsold / **-old** 66
unsound / **-ound** 82
unstable / **-able** 8
unstuck / **-uck** 87
unsung / **-ung** 92
untangle / **-angle** 20
unthread / **-ed** 35
untie / **-i** 45
untied / **-ide** 48
until / **-ill** 52
untold / **-old** 66
untrue / **-oo** 71

unwary / **-airy** 16
unwell / **-ell** 39
unwind / **-ind** 55
unwise / **-ies** 49
unwrap / **-ap** 21
unzip / **-ip** 57
up / **-up** 93
update / **-ate** 25
upend / **-end** 41
uphill / **-ill** 52
upkeep / **-eep** 38
upon / **-on** 68
uppercut / **-ut** 97
upright / **-ight** 51
upriver / **-iver** 60
uproar / **-ore** 76
uproot / **-ute** 98
upset / **-et** 44
upshot / **-ot** 81
upstage / **-age** 13
upstart / **-art** 23
upstream / **-eam** 30
urn / **-urn** 95
us / **-us** 96
use / **-oose** 74
use / **-use** 96
useful / **-ul** 90
usherette / **-et** 44
utmost / **-ost** 80
utter / **-utter** 98
U-turn / **-urn** 94

V

vaccinate / **-ate** 25
vaccine / **-een** 37
vagabond / **-ond** 69
vain / **-ane** 20
valentine / **-ine** 55
valid / **-id** 47
valley / **-alley** 17
valley / **-e** 29
value / **-oo** 71
valued / **-ude** 88
vampire / **-ire** 57
van / **-an** 18
vane / **-ane** 20
vanish / **-ish** 58
various / **-us** 96
vary / **-airy** 16
vast / **-ast** 24
vat / **-at** 24
veer / **-ear** 31
vein / **-ane** 20
vent / **-ent** 41
ventilator / **-ator** 26
venue / **-oo** 71
verse / **-urse** 95
very / **-erry** 42
vest / **-est** 43
vet / **-et** 44
vex / **-ecks** 34
vibrate / **-ate** 25
video / **-o** 61
videos / **-ows** 85
videotape / **-ape** 21
view / **-oo** 70
viewed / **-ude** 88
viewpoint / **-oint** 65
vigil / **-ill** 52
vile / **-ile** 52
vine / **-ine** 55
violin / **-in** 54
VIP / **-e** 29
virus / **-us** 96
visit / **-it** 59
vitamin / **-in** 54
vivid / **-id** 47
volcano / **-o** 61
volcanoes / **-ows** 85
vole / **-ole** 67
volleyball / **-all** 17
volt / **-olt** 67
volunteer / **-ear** 31
voodoo / **-oo** 70
vote / **-oat** 63
vouch / **-ouch** 81
vow / **-ow** 83
vowed / **-oud** 82
vowel / **-owl** 84
vroom / **-oom** 73

W

wade / **-ade** 12
wag / **-ag** 13
wage / **-age** 13
wail / **-ale** 14
waist / **-aced** 9
waistcoat / **-oat** 63
wait / **-ate** 25
waiter / **-ator** 26
wake / **-ake** 16
wakeful / **-ul** 90
walk / **-ork** 78
walkie-talkie / **-e** 29
wall / **-all** 17
wallflower / **-ower** 84
walnut / **-ut** 97
walrus / **-us** 96
wan / **-on** 68
wand / **-ond** 69
wane / **-ane** 20
war / **-ore** 76
ward / **-oard** 62
wardrobe / **-obe** 64
warehouse / **-ouse** 83
warlike / **-ike** 51
warm / **-orm** 78
wars / **-ores** 77
warship / **-ip** 57
wart / **-ort** 79
wary / **-airy** 16
wash / **-osh** 80
waste / **-aced** 9
wasteland / **-and** 19
watchdog / **-og** 65
watchful / **-ul** 90
watchstrap / **-ap** 21
watchtower / **-ower** 84
waterborne / **-orn** 78
watercress / **-ess** 42
waterfall / **-all** 17
waterski / **-e** 29
watertight / **-ight** 51
waterweed / **-eed** 36
wave / **-ave** 27
waveband / **-and** 19
wax / **-acks** 11
waxwork / **-urk** 94
way / **-ay** 27
ways / **-aze** 28
we / **-e** 29
weak / **-eek** 37
wean / **-een** 37
wear / **-air** 15
weathercock / **-ock** 64
weathervane / **-ane** 20
weave / **-eve** 44
website / **-ight** 51
wed / **-ed** 35
wedge / **-edge** 35
Wednesday / **-ay** 27
wee / **-e** 29
weed / **-eed** 36
week / **-eek** 37
weekday / **-ay** 27
weekdays / **-aze** 28
weekender / **-ender** 41
weep / **-eep** 38
weigh / **-ay** 27
weighed / **-ade** 12
weight / **-ate** 25
welcome / **-um** 90
well / **-ell** 39
well-paid / **-ade** 12
went / **-ent** 41
wept / **-ept** 42
were / **-ur** 94
west / **-est** 43
westbound / **-ound** 82
wet / **-et** 44
wetsuit / **-ute** 98
whack / **-ack** 10
whacked / **-act** 11
whacks / **-acks** 11
whale / **-ale** 14
whaling / **-ing** 56
wham / **-am** 17
what / **-ot** 81
wheat / **-eat** 32
wheel / **-eal** 30
wheelbarrow / **-o** 61
wheelchair / **-air** 15
wheeze / **-ees** 38
wheezy / **-easy** 32
whelp / **-elp** 39
when / **-en** 40
where / **-air** 15
which / **-itch** 60
whiff / **-iff** 49
whiffed / **-ift** 50
while / **-ile** 52
whim / **-im** 53
whine / **-ine** 55
whined / **-ind** 55
whip / **-ip** 57
whiplash / **-ash** 23
whirl / **-url** 94
whirligig / **-ig** 50
whirlpool / **-ool** 72
whirlybird / **-urred** 95
whisk / **-isk** 58
white / **-ight** 51
whiteboard / **-oard** 62
whitewash / **-osh** 80
whizz / **-is** 58
who / **-oo** 70

whole / **-ole** 67
wholemeal / **-eal** 30
whoop / **-oop** 74
whose / **-use** 96
why / **-i** 45
wide / **-ide** 48
widespread / **-ed** 35
wife / **-ife** 49
wig / **-ig** 50
wiggle / **-iggle** 50
wigwam / **-am** 17
wild / **-ild** 52
wildcat / **-at** 24
wildfire / **-ire** 57
wildflower / **-ower** 84
wildfowl / **-owl** 84
wildlife / **-ife** 49
will / **-ill** 52
willpower / **-ower** 84
willy-nilly / **-illy** 53
wilt / **-ilt** 53
win / **-in** 54
winch / **-inch** 55
wind / **-ind** 55
windbag / **-ag** 13
windbreak / **-ake** 16
windfall / **-all** 17
windmill / **-ill** 52
window / **-o** 61
windowpane / **-ane** 20
windowsill / **-ill** 52
windpipe / **-ipe** 57
windscreen / **-een** 37
windswept / **-ept** 42
wine / **-ine** 55
wing / **-ing** 56
wingspan / **-an** 18
wink / **-ink** 56
wintertime / **-ime** 54
wipe / **-ipe** 57
wire / **-ire** 57
wisdom / **-um** 90
wise / **-ies** 49
wisecrack / **-ack** 10
wish / **-ish** 58
wishbone / **-one** 69
wishful / **-ul** 90
wit / **-it** 59
witch / **-itch** 60
witchcraft / **-aft** 13
within / **-in** 54
without / **-out** 83
withstand / **-and** 19
withstood / **-ood** 72
wobble / **-obble** 63
woe / **-o** 61
woes / **-ows** 85
woke / **-oke** 66
wombat / **-at** 24
won / **-un** 92
wonder / **-under** 92
wonderful / **-ul** 90
wonderland / **-and** 19
wondrous / **-us** 96
woo / **-oo** 70
wood / **-ood** 72
woodcutter / **-utter** 98
woodpile / **-ile** 52
woodshed / **-ed** 35
woodwork / **-urk** 94
wooed / **-ude** 88
wool / **-ul** 90
word / **-urred** 95
wore / **-ore** 76
work / **-urk** 94
workout / **-out** 83
worksheet / **-eet** 32
workshop / **-op** 75
workspace / **-ace** 9
worldwide / **-ide** 48
worn / **-orn** 78
worse / **-urse** 95
worthwhile / **-ile** 52
would / **-ood** 72
wound / **-ound** 82
wow / **-ow** 83
wowed / **-oud** 82
wrangle / **-angle** 20
wrap / **-ap** 21
wreck / **-eck** 33
wrecked / **-ect** 34
wrecks / **-ecks** 34
wren / **-en** 40
wrench / **-ench** 40
wretch / **-etch** 44
wriggle / **-iggle** 50
wring / **-ing** 56
wrist / **-ist** 58
write / **-ight** 51
writing / **-ing** 56
wrong / **-ong** 69
wrote / **-oat** 63
wrung / **-ung** 92
wry / **-i** 45

X

x-ray / **-ay** 27
x-rayed / **-ade** 12
x-rays / **-aze** 28
xylophone / **-one** 69

y

yacht / **-ot** 81
yak / **-ack** 10
yaks / **-acks** 11
yam / **-am** 17
yank / **-ank** 21
yap / **-ap** 21
yard / **-ard** 22
yawn / **-orn** 78
yearn / **-urn** 94
yeast / **-east** 32
yell / **-ell** 39
yellow / **-ello** 39
yelp / **-elp** 39
yen / **-en** 40
yes / **-ess** 42
yesterday / **-ay** 27
yet / **-et** 44
yippee / **-e** 29
yolk / **-oke** 66
yoo-hoo / **-oo** 70
you / **-oo** 70
young / **-ung** 92
yours / **-ores** 77
yowl / **-owl** 84
yo-yo / **-o** 61
yo-yos / **-ows** 85
yuck / **-uck** 87
yule / **-ool** 72
yum-yum / **-um** 90

z

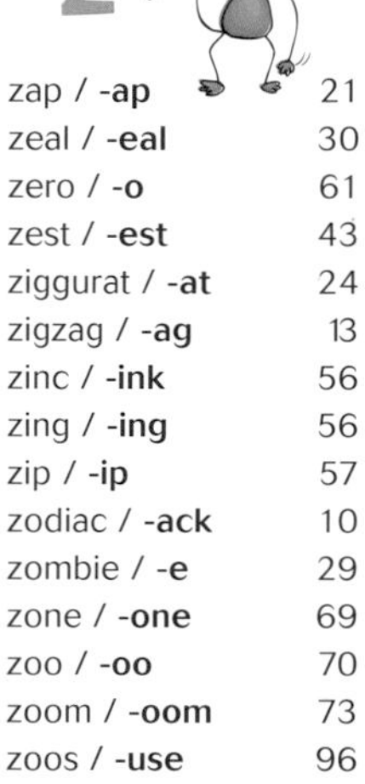

zap / **-ap** 21
zeal / **-eal** 30
zero / **-o** 61
zest / **-est** 43
ziggurat / **-at** 24
zigzag / **-ag** 13
zinc / **-ink** 56
zing / **-ing** 56
zip / **-ip** 57
zodiac / **-ack** 10
zombie / **-e** 29
zone / **-one** 69
zoo / **-oo** 70
zoom / **-oom** 73
zoos / **-use** 96

First published 2003 by A & C Black Publishers Limited
37 Soho Square, London W1D 3QZ
www.acblack.com

Designed by Rachel Hamdi and Holly Mann
Edited by Mary-Jane Wilkins
Illustrations by Sofie Forrester, Sarah Garson, Kate Pankhurst,
Holly Surplice and Sara Wilson

Thanks to Lilian Briggs for her advice.

A CIP record for this book is available from
the British Library.

ISBN 0-7136-6510-6

Typeset in New Contemporary Brush, Cosmos
and Stempel Garamond

Printed in Singapore by Imago

A & C Black uses paper produced with elemental chlorine-free pulp,
harvested from managed sustainable forests.